NEW DIRECTIONS
FOR METHODOLOGY OF
SOCIAL AND
BEHAVIORAL SCIENCE

Number 4 • 1980

NEW DIRECTIONS FOR METHODOLOGY OF SOCIAL AND BEHAVIORAL SCIENCE

A Quarterly Sourcebook
Donald W. Fiske, Editor-in-Chief

Number 4, 1980

Fallible Judgment in Behavioral Research

Richard A. Shweder
Guest Editor

Jossey-Bass Inc., Publishers
San Francisco • Washington • London

FALLIBLE JUDGMENT IN BEHAVIORAL RESEARCH
New Directions for Methodology of Social and Behavioral Science
Number 4, 1980
Richard A. Shweder, Guest Editor

New Directions for Methodology of Social and Behavioral Science is published quarterly by Jossey-Bass Inc., Publishers. Subscriptions are available at the regular rate for institutions, libraries, and agencies of $30 for one year. Individuals may subscribe at the special professional rate of $18 for one year.

Correspondence:
Subscriptions, single-issue orders, change of address notices, undelivered copies, and other correspondence should be sent to *New Directions* Subscriptions, Jossey-Bass Inc., Publishers, 433 California Street, San Francisco, California 94104. Editorial correspondence should be sent to the Editor-in-Chief, Donald W. Fiske, University of Chicago, Chicago, Illinois 60637.

Library of Congress Catalogue Card Number LC 79-89414

Cover design by Willi Baum

Manufactured in the United States of America

Contents

Editor's Notes

How do experts and novices pursue their scientific goals? How do they go about gathering information, evaluating evidence, estimating likelihoods, making predictions, and constructing explanatory theories? In recent years the view has emerged that scientific experts and lay people share a number of statistical and logical intuitions which, in certain respects, are faulty and sometimes even systematically biased. In this sourcebook we examine the limitations of our intuitive scientific procedures and discuss some of the ways these limitations can be overcome.

Hillel J. Einhorn begins the volume with a discussion of outcome irrelevant learning structures (OILS). Einhorn argues that outcome feedback is not a sufficient condition for learning from experience. He examines our unwarranted faith in the accuracy and veracity of our judgments and beliefs and links this overconfidence to (1) our failure to search out and process disconfirming evidence; (2) our unawareness of environmental effects on outcomes; and (3) our reliance on certain biased strategies for gathering, storing, and retrieving outcome information.

Next, Lee Ross and Mark R. Lepper document what they refer to as a "human tendency to cling to existing beliefs," and consider the normative question, under what conditions should our pre-existing beliefs and theories yield to apparently disconfirming evidence?

Richard A. Shweder and Roy G. D'Andrade focus on systematic distortion in person perception, and document a judgmental strategy for producing cognitive illusions. Shweder and D'Andrade argue that on memory-based personality procedures, judges confound likeness in meaning with co-occurrence likelihood, and confuse "propositions about language" with "propositions about the world." They discuss the implications of their systematic distortion hypothesis for our understanding of personality structure, human judgment, and implicit personality theory.

Donald W. Fiske examines the potentials and limitations of verbal report data. He considers the implications of recent challenges to the veridicality of verbal reports and suggests that veridicality "increases with the extent to which the report is of more immediate experience and requires a minimum of cognitive processing."

Robyn M. Dawes discusses the relationship between statistical and clinical inference. Reviewing the evidence on decisions about college admissions, Dawes argues that decisions limited to a few explicit assessment criteria and derived from regression equations do well compared to the intuitive judgments of most admission officers. As Dawes notes, "the whole trick is to know what variables to look at and then to know how to add." Dawes considers the ethical and practical implications of mechanizing decisions about college admissions.

Finally, Baruch Fischhoff examines the difficulties of discerning valid repetitive patterns from historical evidence. Attributed to Kierkegaard is the epigram that "Life is lived forwards but understood backwards." Fischhoff takes a closer look at the relationship between prospects and retrospects.

Richard A. Shweder
Guest Editor

Richard A. Shweder is associate professor on the Committee on Human Development, Department of Behavioral Sciences, University of Chicago. He is a psychological anthropologist trained at Harvard University.

Given that judgment is fallible, our beliefs about our own judgmental ability are likely to be seriously in error.

Overconfidence in Judgment

Hillel J. Einhorn

Three groups of scientists studying the effects of a particular bacterium (X) on a certain disease (Y) reach the following conclusions: Group 1: Although $p(Y|X) \neq 1.0$, it is greater than what could be expected by chance alone—therefore X contributes to causing Y; Group 2: X and Y are unrelated since a toxin given off by various micro-organisms (Z) is confounded with X; Group 3: X and Z are both important determinants of Y but only within a certain temperature range (W). This example illustrates the difficulty of evaluating the meaning of outcome information *even when* there is agreement on the scientific method as the way of gaining knowledge. On the other hand, consider some of your own judgments, beliefs, and hypotheses: for example, you judge your friend Joe to be devious, you believe that honesty is the best policy, you hold the hypothesis that the Democrats are responsible for inflation, and so on. Although our judgments and beliefs may be considered as hypotheses to be tested, we are generally quite confident in their truth without ever formally testing them. This immediately raises a question: if the difficulty of making scientific inferences from evidence is so great, how is it that many of our own judgments, beliefs, and hypotheses are held with such extreme confidence?

The importance of the above question is that it brings into focus the relations between what we know and how we come to know it. In particular, what we know about our judgmental ability is directly related to the way in which we gather, test, and interpret evidence. The argument to be pursued here is that the methods we use to accomplish these goals do not make use of scientific methodology but instead rely on unaided judgment (Hammond, 1978). Therefore, we are in the common but unenviable position of having to continually judge our own judgment. Furthermore, if judgmental biases are as frequent as much research suggests (see Slovic, Fischhoff, and Lichtenstein, 1977, for a review), we must seriously entertain the hypothesis that a great deal of what we believe about our judgmental ability is in error.

The perspective taken in this chapter is that overconfidence in judgment is a result of the way in which outcome feedback is used to evaluate and learn about judgmental accuracy. Moreover, the focus on feedback raises questions about our ability to learn from experience (Brehmer, in press; Einhorn, in press). At a more general level, the issues of how and how well we learn from experience underlie most of what follows. This is explicitly considered in the first section and thereafter the concept of outcome irrelevant learning structures (OILS) is introduced. A typology of OILS is presented, as are various examples. Finally, a brief discussion of improving our ability to learn about judgment is provided.

Judgment, Choice, and Learning from Experience

The ubiquity of judgment is obvious; we are continually forced to evaluate and interpret information as well as to predict future consequences of actions. For example, in reading thus far, you have made many judgments regarding whether this paper is interesting, useful, understandable, and so on. Furthermore, whether you continue reading or not, you have made a prediction about the likely benefits and costs of either action. Note that the linkage of judgment and choice is particularly important since judgment can play an important role in aiding choice (Einhorn, Kleinmuntz, and Kleinmuntz, 1979). Moreover, since one has to choose what action to take in order to satisfy basic needs and wants, it is essential for any organism to learn the degree to which actions lead to desirable or undesirable outcomes. This means that a great deal of learning from experience must involve the learning of judgment-action-outcome linkages.

How does one know that one has made an accurate judgment or a good decision? The obvious answer is that one looks at outcomes to judge the quality of inputs. The reinforcement value of feedback is central to learning. As Powers (1973, p. 351) has pointed out: "All behavior involves strong feedback effects, whether one is considering spinal reflexes or self-actualization. Feedback is such an all-pervasive and fundamental aspect of behavior that it is as invisable as the air we breathe. Quite literally it is behavior—we know nothing of our own behavior but the feedback effects of our own outputs." In addition to the frequency of reinforcement via feedback, outcome feedback is visible, available, and usually unambiguous. In fact, it is difficult to think of any other way to evaluate judgments and decisions. However, formal decision theory does offer a different way: namely, that the *process* of deciding be such that one maximizes expected utility. Therefore, outcomes do not necessarily provide a criterion for judging the quality of decisions. While the distinction between the quality of outcomes and the quality of decisions is useful, it is difficult to accept since we have learned to evaluate decisions by their outcomes.

Although the statement just made may seem obvious, the implications regarding the ability to learn about our judgment are not. Specifically, what are the effects of being correct (positive outcome) for the wrong reasons (that is, being right *in spite of* one's judgment) and being wrong for the right reasons? This question indicates that outcomes result from a variety of factors, not all of which are under our control or even within our awareness. Therefore, the use of outcome feedback is not without its problems in providing a self-correcting mechanism for improving judgment. In fact, feedback can be self-destroying if it is erroneously interpreted (Bandura, 1978; Seligman, 1975). In order to provide a clear view of the judgment-choice-outcome process, a schematic representation is shown in Figure 1 (from Einhorn and Hogarth, 1978).

First consider Boxes (1)–(4). Note that outcomes follow from our initial judgments and predictions (1), which are then used to determine actions and choices (2). However, this occurs within a particular environment (3), which refers to all of the factors that can influence the outcome; that is, structural characteristics of the task, such as the amount of random variation. The environment is so pervasive that, like the statement by Powers concerning feedback, it is "as invisible as the air we breathe." However, it is the combination of judgments, actions, and environments that produce outcomes. Consequently, outcome feedback will pass to either or both of Boxes (1) and (2) but, in the absence of adequate control or understanding of (3), inferences regarding relations between judgments, actions, and outcomes remain problematic. It should be noted that the formation of formal hypotheses and the use of experiments does lead to more interpretable outcomes for exactly the reason that the environment is specified and controlled.

Although the importance of the environment in affecting outcomes is substantial, awareness of the role of environmental factors is typically low (Ross, 1977). The lack of awareness of so crucial a set of factors is related to a distinction between the *content* and the *structure* of tasks. Content refers to the substantive aspects of the task, including the various details, while structure refers to the more general principles that underlie the task. Since much of learning from experience involves induction via specific cases, the content of tasks may hide their structure, making learning difficult. An interesting example of this is provided by Simon and Hayes (1976) regarding what they call "problem isomorphs." They have shown that different surface wordings of structurally identical problems (problems that can be solved using identical principles) greatly changes how people represent the problem in memory and consequently solve it. Therefore concern with the way content can affect the perception of outcomes is important in fully understanding feedback effects and this is shown by Boxes (5) and (6) in Figure 1. Note that outcomes must be coded and stored in memory, and then retrieved when needed. Furthermore, the way in which coded outcomes are evaluated and used for making inferences (6) is also important. Therefore, the more complete picture of feedback involves Boxes (1)–(6), and emphasizes both the factors that influence outcomes and the person's perception and understanding of this process.

Figure 1. Schematic Representation of Judgment-Action-Outcome Situation

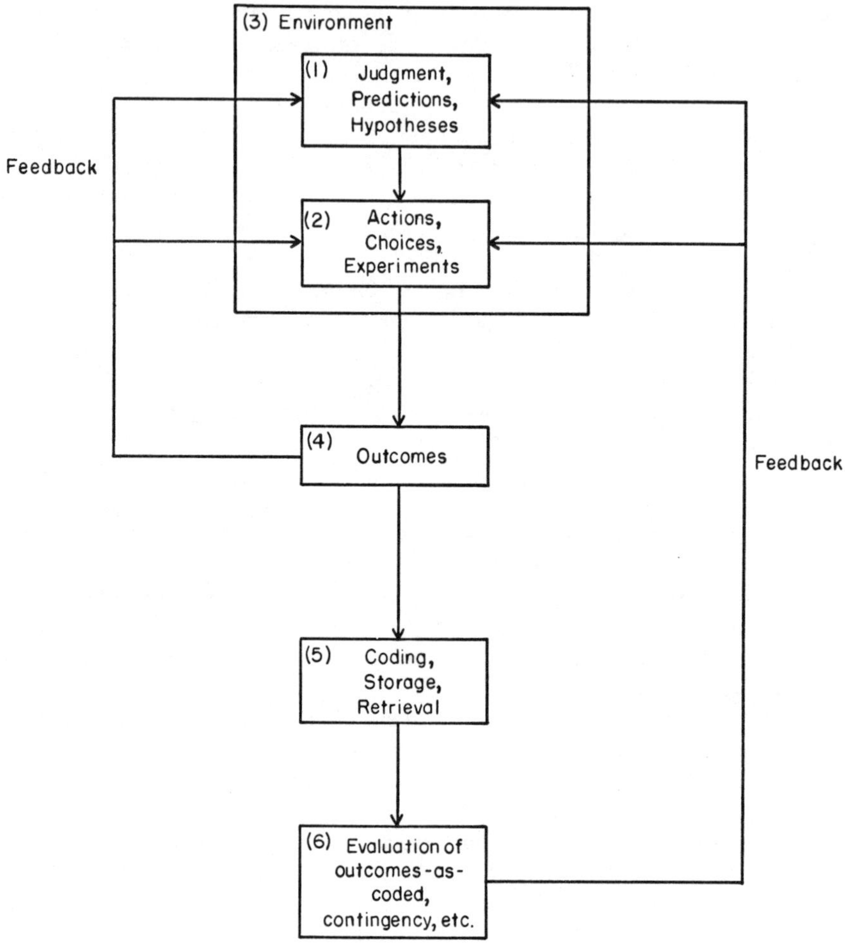

OILS

The main argument of this chapter is now presented by considering the concept of *o*utcome *i*rrelevant *l*earning *s*tructures (OILS) (Einhorn, in press). This means that in certain tasks outcome feedback can be irrelevant and even harmful for correcting poor judgment, incorrect beliefs, and false hypotheses. Moreover, positive outcome feedback without knowledge of task structure tends to keep us unaware that our judgment is poor since there is very little motivation to question how successes were achieved. (This is illustrated by the adage, "If it works, leave it alone.")

Before offering a typology of OILS, an example of what is meant is given within a shopping context. Imagine shopping in the supermarket and coming to cans of juice with the following prices and overall quality (adapted from Tversky, 1969):

Brand	*Price*	*Quality*
X	60¢	High
Y	55¢	Medium
Z	50¢	Low

Assume that I use the following rule to choose among the three brands: If the price difference is 5¢ or less, choose the brand with the higher quality; if the price difference is greater than 5¢, choose according to price. Such a simple rule (which is a lexicographic semiorder) leads to:

$$X > Y$$
$$Y > Z \text{, but}$$
$$Z > X$$

Therefore this rule leads to intransitive choices, which is considered irrational since it leads to a "money pump." For example, if you had X but prefer Z, you should be willing to give up X for Z and pay a fee for your preferred choice. But note that the same idea holds for trading Z for Y, and then Y for X. You have now paid three fees but end up with X, where the process can start over. Note, however, that after I choose X over Y, I may then eliminate Y from the remaining set and compare X with Z. Therefore, I end up with Z, which may be quite acceptable after I taste it. I then congratulate myself on what a good shopper I am—I saved money and got a reasonable product. The important point to note here is that by not making the Y versus Z comparison, I remain unaware that my rule leads to an intransitive choice. All I *am* aware of is that I made a choice with minimal fuss and strain and the outcome was satisfactory. Therefore, positive outcome feedback reinforces a normatively poor rule, and there is no awareness that something is wrong.

A typology for categorizing various OILS is now presented and discussed below. This typology is shown in Table 1.

Table 1. Typology of Outcome Irrelevant Learning Structures (OILS)

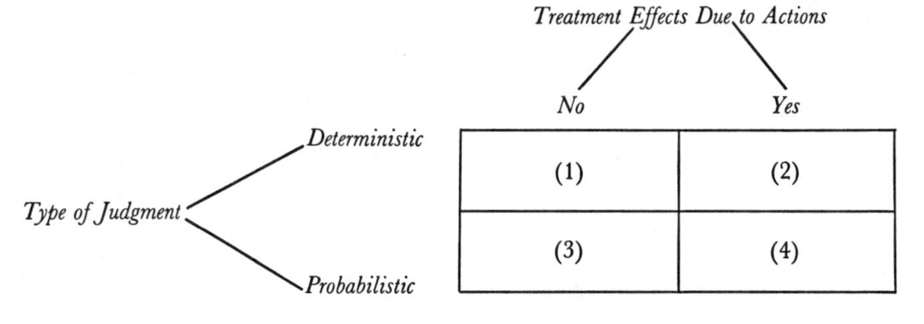

Judgments have been divided according to whether they are deterministic or probabilistic. The latter is defined here as any judgment or prediction that has given probability or odds statement connected with it; for instance, a horse is 3:1 to win a race (meaning that its probability of winning is .25). All other judgments that do not contain an uncertainty statement shall be considered deterministic. The second factor to consider is whether there are "treatment effects" due to the action or choice. This is best illustrated by an example, although the formal structure will be discussed later. Imagine that you are a waiter in a busy restaurant and because you cannot give good service to all the people at your station, you make a judgment regarding which people will leave good or poor tips. You then give good or bad service depending on your judgment. If the quality of service, *in itself,* has an effect on the size of the tip, outcome feedback will "confirm" the predictions ("they looked cheap and left no tip—just as I thought"). The extent of such self-fulfilling prophecies is much greater than we think and represents a considerable obstacle to learning from outcome feedback. However, before considering this in detail, let us look at Cell 1 for the general structure of the tasks to be discussed.

Deterministic Judgments, No Treatment Effects

The task to be discussed is one in which an overall, evaluative judgment (x) is made for the purpose of choosing between alternative actions, A and B. Furthermore, let x_c be a cutoff point such that,

$$\begin{aligned} &\text{if } x \geq x_c, \text{ take action A;} \\ &\text{if } x < x_c, \text{ take action B.} \end{aligned} \qquad (1)$$

Although simplistic, Equation (1) applies to many judgment/decision situations, for example: job hiring, promotion, admission to school, loan and credit granting, assignment to remedial programs, admission to social programs, journal article acceptance, grant awarding, and so on. In these cases, a judgment of the degree of "deservedness" typically determines which action is to be taken since the preferred action cannot be given to all.

In order to compare judgment to a standard, the existence of a criterion, denoted y, is assumed to serve as the basis for evaluating the accuracy of judgment. While the practical difficulties of finding and developing adequate criteria are enormous, it is the concept of a criterion which is necessary for this analysis. To be consistent with the formulation of judgment, it is further assumed that the criterion has a cutoff point (y_c) such that $y \geq y_c$ and $y < y_c$ serve as the basis for evaluating the outcomes of judgment. Thus, as far as learning about judgment is concerned, representation of outcomes in memory is often of categorical form, that is, successes and failures (Estes, 1976).

The formal structure of this task can be seen by considering the regression of y on x and the four quadrants that result from the intersection of x_c and y_c as illustrated in Figure 2. Denote the correct predictions positive and negative hits, and the two types of errors, false positives ($y < y_c | x \geq x_c$) and false negatives ($y \geq y_c | x < x_c$). To estimate the relationship between x and y (the

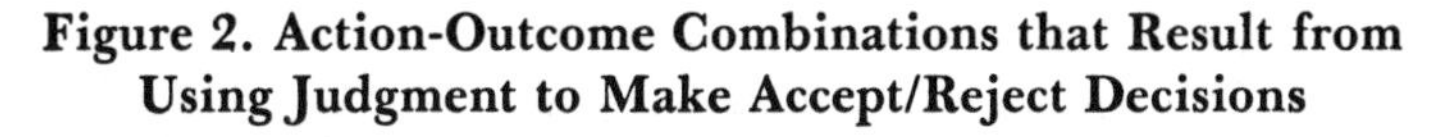

Figure 2. Action-Outcome Combinations that Result from Using Judgment to Make Accept/Reject Decisions

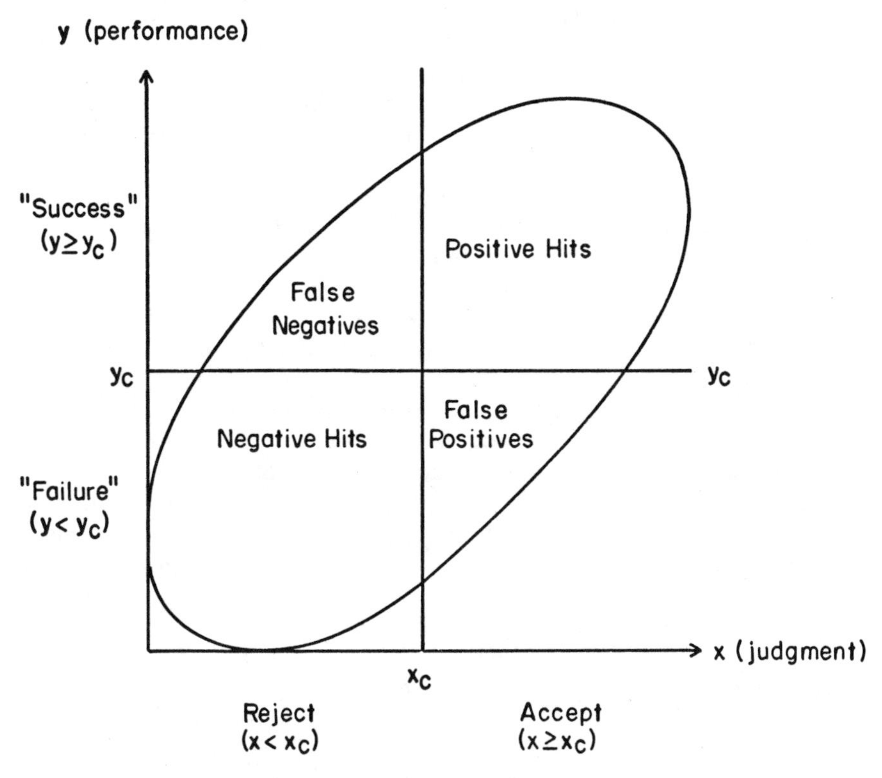

correlation between x and y, r_{xy}) it is necessary to have information on *each* judgment–outcome combination. Assume first that such information becomes available over time (sequentially) and consider the experimental evidence concerned with learning the relationship between x and y in such circumstances. Research on the ability to judge the contingency between x and y from information in 2 x 2 tables (Jenkins and Ward, 1965; Rothbart, in press; Shweder, 1977; Smedslund, 1963, 1966; Ward and Jenkins, 1965) indicates that people judge the strength of relationship by the frequency of positive hits (in the terminology of Figure 2), while generally ignoring information in the three other cells. These results are extremely important since they say that *even* when all of the relevant outcome information is available, people do not use it. This means that in laboratory studies which have outcome *relevant* learning structures, people have transformed them into OILS. How can this be explained?

The argument advanced here concerns the difficulty people have in making use of discomfirming information, that is, the information that can be gained by the nonoccurrence of an action or prediction. Furthermore, a principal cause of this difficulty is the structure of judgmental tasks in the natural environment, since this determines the conditions in which inferential learning can occur. For example, in Figure 2, note that outcomes for those judged below x_c are rarely visible, while outcomes for those who are accepted are the focus of attention. Consequently, it is suggested that habits regarding the lack of search for disconfirming evidence are learned through experience of inferential tasks in naturalistic settings (also see Rothbart, in press, for a discussion of attentional issues in contingency judgments).

The lack of search for disconfirming evidence has been shown in a number of important experimental studies. In an early study, Wason (1960) presented subjects with a three number sequence, for example, 2, 4, 6. Subjects were required to discover the rule to which the three numbers conformed (the rule being three ascending numbers). To discover the rule, they were permitted to generate sets of three numbers that the experimenter classified as conforming or not conforming to the rule. At any point, subjects could stop when they thought they had discovered the rule. The correct solution to this task should involve a search for disconfirming evidence rather than the accumulation of confirming evidence. For example, if someone believed that the rule had something to do with even numbers, this could only be tested by trying a sequence involving an odd number (accumulating vast amounts of confirming instances of even number sequences would not lead to the rule). The fact that only six of twenty-nine subjects found the correct rule the first time they thought they did illustrates the dangers of induction by simple enumeration. As Wason (1960) points out, the solution to this task must involve "a willingness to attempt to falsify hypotheses, and thus to *test those intuitive ideas which so often carry the feelings of certitude*" (p. 139, emphasis added).

A second series of experiments by Wason (1968, 1969) provides further insight into how people search for information to verify inferences (see also Wason and Johnson-Laird, 1972). Subjects were presented with four cards on which one letter or number appeared (a, b, 2, or 3). They were then told to verify the statement "All cards with a vowel on one side have an even number on the other" by indicating only those cards that would need to be turned over in order to determine whether the rule was true or false. Most subjects chose Cards a and 2 or Card a alone instead of the correct response of Cards a and 3.

In addition to the experimental evidence cited above, ask yourself whether you have searched for discomfirming evidence to test the validity of some of your strongest beliefs. For example, do you regularly subscribe to and read newspapers and magazines that are diametrically opposed to your own political views? Do you actively seek out people of hostile religious beliefs to test your own convictions? Most of us (including myself) do not do this and so we act in a nonscientific (but more comfortable) way. Therefore, although we may seek disconfirming evidence in our own scientific work, few of us have set up our own beliefs and personal theories as hypotheses to be rejected on the basis of disconfirming evidence. Furthermore, the difficulty of engaging in these activities in underlined by noting that the testing of hypotheses via disconfirming evidence is a relatively recent occurrence. For example, the concept of a control group, which is essential to scientific method and which illustrates the necessity of nonoccurrence (no treatment) for making valid inferences, came rather late in the history of thought (Boring, 1954; also see Gillis and Schneider, 1966). Popper's (1959) views that hypotheses can only be disconfirmed by evidence but never confirmed have also only recently gained acceptance. People do not search for disconfirming evidence. That does not mean that they ignore outcome feedback, only that they selectively attend to certain aspects of it. For example, if there are many false positives as compared with positive hits, this is evidence that our judgment is inaccurate. However, the absence of false positives is *not* evidence that our judgment is accurate (if P implies Q, not-P does not imply not-Q). In fact, one can have very few false positives even when judgment is poor—the reason being that outcomes are also determined by environmental factors (if you forgot this, go back to Figure 1, Box 3).

In order to illustrate, first note that the number of positive hits relative to the number of false positives is equal to the ratio of the positive hits to the positive *rates;* that is, $p(y \geq y_c | x \geq x_c)/p(y < y_c | x \geq x_c)$. This is shown as follows:

$$\text{No. of positive hits} = (\text{No. of applicants})\begin{pmatrix}\text{proportion}\\ \text{selected}\end{pmatrix}(\text{positive hit rate})$$

$$\text{No. of false positives} = (\text{No. of applicants})\begin{pmatrix}\text{proportion}\\ \text{selected}\end{pmatrix}(\text{false positive rate})$$

$$\text{Therefore, the ratio, } \frac{\text{No. of positive hits}}{\text{No. of false positives}} = \frac{\text{positive hit rate}}{\text{false positive rate}}$$

Furthermore, these two conditional probabilities are complements so that as one goes up the other goes down. Now consider Figure 2 again and note that three factors will influence the positive hit rate/false positive ratio: the correlation between x and y (which determines the slope of the regression line), the placement of x_c, and the placement of y_c. For a given value of r_{xy} and y_c, note that if one increases x_c by moving it to the right, the positive hit rate increases and the false positive rate decreases (indeed, there is a point at which the false positive rate is zero). Therefore, by being more selective (reducing the probability of $x \geq x_c$, which is called the selection ratio) one can receive positive outcome feedback regarding one's judgmental ability even if r_{xy} is low. In fact, it was noted quite early in industrial testing situations (Taylor and Russell, 1939) that one could set x_c to achieve any desired positive hit rate, given particular values of r_{xy} and the base rate, $p(y \geq y_c)$. (This is not true in the limiting case of $r_{xy} = 0$).

A second consideration in evaluating feedback in tasks like the above is being aware of the base rate itself: what percentage of people will be above y_c if one *randomly* assigned people to actions A and B? If people ignore base rates, as much evidence suggests (see Bar-Hillel, in press; Lyon and Slovic, 1976; Tversky and Kahneman, 1974), the difficulty of making correct inferences from outcome feedback is further increased. For example, consider a person who experiences an 80 percent positive hit rate. Without knowledge of the base rate, this hit rate may seem to be indicative of accurate judgment. However, if the base rate were 70 percent, the 80 percent hit rate would not look as impressive. Therefore, accuracy of judgment should be evaluated as the marginal increase in the hit rate over the base rate. If people do not use the marginal hit rate to evaluate their judgment, they are likely to overestimate their judgmental ability.

Deterministic Judgment, Treatment Effects

Treatment effects due to actions are now considered in the context of the task discussed in the preceding section. To begin, imagine the following experiment: Assume a series a judgments is made about some persons; of those judged to be above x_c, randomly assign half to Action A and half to Action B. Similarly, do the same for those judged below x_c. At some later time, measure performance and calculate the proportion of those with $y \geq y_c$ in each cell (each person is assigned a 0 or 1 to indicate whether he or she is below or above the cutoff on y, the proportion above y_c being simply the mean of that cell). This is a 2 × 2 factorial design, with one factor being "judgment" and the other factor, "type of action." Note that people receiving Actions A and B have also received different experimental treatments.

If this experiment were done, one could test for the main effect of judgment (which measures its accuracy); the main effect for the action, that is, whether receiving Action A or B in itself causes differences in performance; and the interaction between judgment and action. Observe that the advantage of the experiment is that it allows one to untangle the accuracy of judgment from the treatment effects of the action. However, such an experiment is rarely done, even conceptually and especially not by people without extensive training in experimental design. Therefore, judgmental accuracy will almost always be confounded with possible treatment effects due to actions. Furthermore, this experiment allows one to examine disconfirming information. Therefore, in contrast to most real judgmental tasks, it would permit one to disconfirm the hypothesis of judgmental accuracy as well as to estimate any treatment effects due to actions.

To illustrate how treatment effects may increase confidence in judgment, consider the decision to award grants to researchers. Assume that grant applications are judged on some basis of potential, where those judged above x_c receive rewards and those judged below x_c are denied. Assume also that the granting agency wishes to determine whether its judging procedures produce satisfactory results. To this end, it develops a criterion that reflects both quantity and quality of completed research. It then examines funded projects and calculates the proportion considered successes. If the proportion of successes for those given grants is high, the agency might feel that its judgmental procedures are quite accurate. However, note that the treatment effect of receiving a grant is completely confounded with judgmental accuracy, for example, obtaining a grant can give a researcher time and resources to do more and better work. If there were a main effect for the action (in the direction assumed here), one might still experience a high positive hit rate, even if the accuracy of the judgment were low (or perhaps zero). Note that the proper experiment would be difficult to do, since it would require withholding grants from some "deserving" cases while awarding grants to some who do not "deserve" them. Consequently, the assumed validity of judgment can be continually reinforced by outcome feedback.

When treatment effects are added to the three other factors that influence positive hits (see preceding section), outcome feedback is almost invariably favorable (for a formal statistical model demonstrating this, see Einhorn and Hogarth, 1978). However, it is important to note that the magnitude of treatment effects will be determined to some degree by the nature of the task. For example, if one judges that rain is likely and then bases action on that judgment by carrying an umbrella, it seems absurd to consider that carrying the umbrella can have any effect on the chances of rain. However, in other situations, treatment effects due to actions can be substantial without awareness of their influence. The most compelling evidence of this occurs in medicine and is commonly known as the "placebo effect" (Shapiro, 1960). However, the discovery that any action, no matter how worthless from a pharmacological point of view, can improve patients was very slow in developing. In fact, the invention of placebo control groups is a twentieth century idea.

Although actions and environments can affect outcomes so that we receive confounded feedback in evaluating our judgment, it is possible that judgments and hypotheses can affect activities such as experiments in ways that bias the outcomes. For example, Rosenthal (1966) found that experimenters holding a particular hypothesis have a greater chance of confirming their hypotheses than those holding contrary positions. This clearly points to the difficulty of separating judgments from actions in interpreting outcomes.

Probabilistic Judgment

Consider that you judge the probability of some event to be .70 and assume that the event does not occur. What does the outcome tell you about the accuracy of your judgment? One can argue that any single outcome is irrelevant since a judgment of .70 means that the event should *not* occur 30 percent of the time. In fact, if events to which we give a probability of .70 always occur, this is evidence that the judgment is not very good. Therefore, the criterion for assessing the accuracy of probabilistic judgments must be different from deterministic judgments.

One criterion that has been suggested is that such judgments be "calibrated," by which is meant that judgments at a given probability level match the actual relative frequency of occurence. For example, if I estimated 100 events to each have a probability of .7, 70 of them should have occurred. Note that it is only by keeping a "boxscore" of the relative frequency of outcomes when one judges events with a given probability that one can get useful feedback from outcomes. However, this is likely to be a necessary but not sufficient condition for making well-calibrated judgments. First, over what time period does one keep the boxscore before deciding that the judgment is or is not calibrated? Furthermore, how close is "close enough" in order to say that the judgment is accurate (in the sense of being well calibrated)? Note that this whole mode of evaluating outcomes involves reinforcement that is delayed for long time periods. Therefore, it is not clear that such feedback will have much of a self-correcting effect. Second, in order to improve one's rules for making probability judgments, one's boxscore must include not only one's estimates and the resulting outcomes, but also one's rules for deriving those estimates. For example, if I kept a record of outcomes that resulted for 100 cases in which I gave estimates of .7, what would the feedback that the event happened 53 of those times tell me about the quality of the judgmental rules I used? Since it is likely that many different rules could have been used to estimate probabilities in the 100 different situations, the outcome information is irrelevant and outcome feedback is not useful unless one is both aware of one's rules and a record is kept of their use (consider Nisbett and Wilson, 1977, on whether we are aware of our own cognitive processes).

The above does not imply that it is impossible to learn to make well calibrated probability judgments. If one makes *many* probability judgments in the *same situation,* (as do weather forecasters and horse racing handicappers) and outcome feedback is quickly received, such conditions may not be outcome irrelevant, and feedback can be self-correcting. However, such conditions would seem to be the exception rather than the rule for most of us. Therefore most probability judgments involve OILS, and feedback is not generally self-correcting. In fact, the empirical evidence on calibration (Lichtenstein, Fischhoff, and Phillips, 1977) shows that most people are not well calibrated. Moreover, the lack of calibration is in the direction of overconfidence (Fischhoff, Slovic, and Lichtenstein, 1977): people assign higher probabilities to events than are warranted by empirical relative frequencies.

Finally, an example of treatment effects in probability judgments is offered. The example also has the virtue of showing how difficult it is to discern the structure of tasks when the content is rich in detail. Imagine that you are a military general in a politically tense area and you are concerned about an enemy invasion. Furthermore, from past experience it is known that when enemy troops mass at the border, the probability of invasion is .75. However, you do not have direct access to information about enemy troops but must rely on a report of such activity by your intelligence sources. As it turns out, everytime your intelligence sources report that troops are massing, they are really there. Consider that you now receive a report from your sources that enemy troops are at the border. What is the probability of invasion? More formally, let

H = hypothesis of being invaded
D = troops massing at the border
D* = report of troops massing at the border

The problem states that $p(H|D) = .75$ and $p(D|D^*) = 1.0$, and asks you for $p(H|D^*)$. If you are like most people, you probably answered .75. However, the information given is not sufficient to answer the question in the statistically correct way. In fact, it is possible that in the above problem, $p(H|D^*) = 0$. Since most people find this difficult to believe, consider Figure 3, which illustrates the problem by means of a Venn diagram.

Note that the intersection of H with D* is null, so that the conditional probability, $p(H|D^*)$, is zero. The reason that people find this result so surprising is that they have made a logical fallacy of the form: if D* implies D, then D implies D*. Although D occurs whenever D* is given, the reverse is not necessarily the case. In fact, an intuitive way to see the issue is to think that the enemy is particularly cunning so that your intelligence sources see their troops only when there is no invasion planned. However, when an invasion is planned and troops are at the border, they are hidden so that your sources do not report them.

Let us assume that the general makes the logical error of affirming the consequent and judges the probability of war to be at least .75. He then sends *his* troops to the border thereby causing an invasion by the enemy. Therefore, the faulty reasoning of the general is reinforced by outcome feedback.

Improving the Ability to Learn About Judgment

The difficulty of learning about judgment has been traced to three main factors: (1) lack of search for and use of disconfirming evidence, (2) lack of awareness of environmental effects on outcomes, and (3) the use of unaided memory for coding, storing, and retrieving outcome information. What, if anything, can be done to alleviate these problems? With regard to the use of disconfirming evidence, formal training in experimental design, teaching the

Figure 3. Venn Diagram Showing the Relations Between the Hypothesis (H), Datum (D), and Report of the Datum (D*)

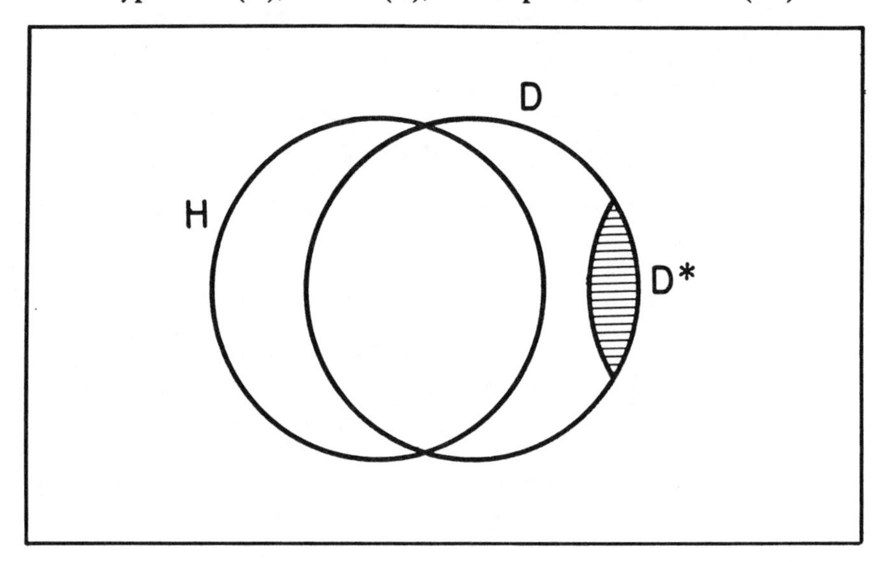

logic of control groups and baseline predictions, and so on would seem to be a necessary but not sufficient condition. Moreover, in order to gain awareness of the environmental effects on outcomes, the use of a model of the environment, as advocated by Hammond and his colleagues (Hammond, Mumpower, and Smith, 1977), has much to recommend it. Such models draw attention to the structure of the environment and the manner in which structure affects outcomes. Finally, is there any way of improving one's memory for outcomes? Since the interval between outcomes and judgments may be large, memory can be considerably aided by simply keeping a box score (Goldberg, 1968). This also has the advantage of keeping a record of disconfirming instances. Moreover, memory can be aided so that it is not only categoric. Tversky and Kahneman (1974) have suggested that people should attempt to encode events not only by their substantive content but by judged probability. When events are grouped in this manner, it is possible to keep a tally of the extent to which judged probabilities match subsequent empirical relative frequencies.

Although the above factors should help to improve learning about judgment, a major obstacle still remains. Recall the example of the waiter making judgments and taking action that results in self-fulfilling prophecies. Now imagine that the waiter was made fully aware of the task structure and the importance of searching for disconfirming evidence. Therefore, he could perform the needed 2 × 2 experiment in order to disentangle judgment from the treatment effects of the action. However, note that he must give good service to some of those judged to leave poor tips and poor service to some judged to leave good tips. Note that the waiter must be willing to risk the possible loss of income *if* his judgment is accurate, against learning that his judgment is poor. Therefore, there is an important trade-off between short-run strategies for action that result in reasonably good outcomes versus long-run strategies for learning that may result in short-run sacrifices. That is, would you be willing to risk the loss of income by doing a real experiment in order to learn? This dilemma confronts us quite often, yet it is not clear that if one was aware of the choice, one would choose to learn. In fact, at the societal level, such experiments may be considered unethical (for example, one could give a remedial program to some of those judged not to need it and withhold it from some of those judged most in need). Therefore, in a great many instances, ethical considerations prevent effective learning and help to maintain an illusion of validity. Exactly *why* it is "unethical" to learn about judgment is not clear. Perhaps overconfidence in judgment is in some way functional—lack of confidence in judgment might result in too much analysis and a crippling of the ability to make quick choices. On the other hand, overconfidence in judgment is related to the perpetuation of myths, magic, and superstitions (Shweder, 1977). The fact that such phenomena serve an important function, and are thus difficult to dispel, should not blind us to the long-run harm they can do. Thus it is fitting to conclude this discussion by quoting from the American humorist Will Rogers: "It's not what we don't know that gives us trouble. It's what we know that ain't so."

References

Bandura, A. "The Self-System in Reciprocal Determinism." *American Psychologist,* 1978, *33,* 344–358.

Bar-Hillel, M. "The Base-Rate Fallacy in Probability Judgments." *Acta Psychologica,* in press.

Boring, E. G. "The Nature and History of Experimental Control." *American Journal of Psychology,* 1954, *67,* 573–589.

Brehmer, B. "Decision Making and Experience." *Conference on Utility and Subjective Probability.* Gothenberg, Sweden, in press.

Einhorn, H. J. "Learning from Experience and Suboptimal Rules in Decision Making." In T. Wallsten (Ed.), *Cognitive Processes in Choice and Decision Behavior.* Hillsdale, N.J.: Erlbaum, in press.

Einhorn, H. J., and Hogarth, R. M. "Confidence in Judgment: Persistence of the Illusion of Validity." *Psychological Review,* 1978, *85,* 395–416.

Einhorn, H. J., Kleinmuntz, D. N., and Kleinmuntz, B. "Linear Regression and Process-Tracing Models of Judgment." *Psychological Review,* 1979, *86,* 465–485.

Estes, W. K. "The Cognitive Side of Probability Learning." *Psychological Review,* 1976, *83,* 37–64.

Fischhoff, B., Slovic, P., and Lichtenstein, S. "Knowing with Certainty: The Appropriateness of Extreme Confidence." *Journal of Experimental Psychology: Human Perception and Performance,* 1977, *3,* 552–564.

Gillis, J., and Schneider, C. "The Historical Preconditions of Representative Design." In K. R. Hammond (Ed.), *The Psychology of Egon Brunswik.* New York: Holt, Rinehart and Winston, 1966.

Goldberg, L. R. "Simple Models or Simple Processes? Some Research on Clinical Judgments." *American Psychologist,* 1968, *23,* 483–496.

Hammond, K. R. "Toward Increasing Competence of Thought in Public Policy Formation." In K. R. Hammond (Ed.), *Judgment and Decision in Public Policy Formation.* Denver, Colo.: Westview Press, 1978.

Hammond, K. R., Mumpower, J. L., and Smith, T. H. "Linking Environmental Models with Models of Human Judgment: A Symmetrical Decision Aid." *IEEE Transactions on Systems, Man, and Cybernetics,* 1977, SMC-7(5), 358–367.

Jenkins, H. M., and Ward, W. C. "Judgment of Contingency Between Responses and Outcomes." *Psychological Monographs: General and Applied,* 1965, *79* (1), whole No. 594.

Lichtenstein, S., Fischhoff, B., and Phillips, L. D. "Calibration of Probabilities: The State of the Art." In H. Jungermann and G. de Zeeuw (Eds.), *Decision Making and Change in Human Affairs.* Dordrecht, The Netherlands: Reidel, 1977.

Lyon, D., and Slovic, P. "Dominance of Accuracy Information and Neglect of Base Rates in Probability Estimation." *Acta Psychologica,* 1976, *40,* 287–298.

Nisbett, R. E., and Wilson, T. D. "Telling More Than We Can Know: Verbal Reports on Mental Processes." *Psychological Review,* 1977, *84,* 231–259.

Popper, K. R. *The Logic of Scientific Discovery.* London, England: Hutchinson, 1959.

Powers, W. T. "Feedback: Beyond Behaviorism." *Science,* 1973, *179,* 351–356.

Rosenthal, R. *Experimenter Effects in Behavioral Research.* New York: Appleton-Century-Crofts, 1966.

Ross, L. "The Intuitive Psychologist and His Shortcomings: Distortions in the Attribution Process." In L. Berkowitz (Ed.), *Advances in Experimental Social Psychology,* 10. New York: Academic Press, 1977.

Rothbart, M. "Memory Processes and Social Beliefs." In D. Hamilton (Ed.), *Cognitive Processes in Stereotyping and Inter-Group Perception.* Hillsdale, N.J.: Erlbaum, in press.

Seligman, M. E. P. *Helplessness. On Depression, Development, and Death.* San Francisco: W. H. Freeman, 1975.

Shapiro, A. K. "A Contribution to a History of the Placebo Effect." *Behavioral Science,* 1960, *5,* 109–135.
Shweder, R. A. "Likeness and Likelihood in Everyday Thought: Magical Thinking in Judgments about Personality." *Current Anthropology,* 1977, *18,* 637–658.
Simon, H. A., and Hayes, J. R. "The Understanding Process: Problem Isomorphs." *Cognitive Psychology,* 1976, *8,* 165–190.
Slovic, P., Fischhoff, B., and Lichtenstein, S. "Behavorial Decision Theory." *Annual Review of Psychology,* 1977, *28,* 1–39.
Smedslund, J. "The Concept of Correlation in Adults." *Scandinavian Journal of Psychology,* 1963, *4,* 165–173.
Smedslund, J. "Note on Learning, Contingency, and Clinical Experience." *Scandinavian Journal of Psychology,* 1966, *7,* 265–266.
Taylor, H. C., and Russell, J. T. "The Relationship of Validity Coefficients to the Practical Effectiveness of Tests in Selection: Discussion and Tables." *Journal of Applied Psychology,* 1939, *23,* 565–578.
Tversky, A. "Intransitivity of Preferences." *Psychological Review,* 1969, *76,* 31–48.
Tversky, A., and Kahneman, D. "Judgment Under Uncertainty: Heuristics and Biases." *Science,* 1974, *185,* 1124–1131.
Ward, W. C., and Jenkins, H. M. "The Display of Information and the Judgment of Contingency." *Canadian Journal of Psychology,* 1965, *19,* 231–241.
Wason, P. C. "On the Failure to Eliminate Hypotheses in a Conceptual Task." *Quarterly Journal of Experimental Psychology,* 1960, *12,* 129–140.
Wason, P. C. "Reasoning About a Rule." *Quarterly Journal of Experimental Psychology,* 1968, *20,* 273–281.
Wason, P. C. "Regression in Reasoning?" *British Journal of Psychology,* 1969, *60,* 471–480.
Wason, P. C., and Johnson-Laird, P. N. *Psychology of Reasoning. Structure and Content.* London, England: Batsford, 1972.

Hillel J. Einhorn is professor of Behavioral Science in the Graduate School of Business and Department of Behavioral Sciences, and director of the Center for Decision Research, University of Chicago.

When and why do our impressions and beliefs survive potent challenges to their validity? How can we improve inferential practice in assimilating data to theories and in accommodating theories to data?

The Perseverance of Beliefs: Empirical and Normative Considerations

Lee Ross
Mark R. Lepper

Three and a half centuries ago, Francis Bacon decried the human tendency to maintain preconceived beliefs in the face of seemingly overwhelming logical or empirical challenges to their validity. Few complaints about human frailty are as consistently confirmed by everyday experience. We are continually confronted with the perversity of friends and colleagues who, despite our best efforts to enlighten them, persist in misguided political, social, and even scientific beliefs; just as they find us, no doubt, intractable and obstinate in our own preconceptions. Empirical research similarly supports Bacon's (1960 [1620]) critique. Opinions (Abelson, 1959; Luchins, 1942, 1957), personality impressions (Asch, 1946; Jones and Goethals, 1971), decisions (Janis, 1968), and a variety of racial, religious, ethnic, and sex role stereotypes (Allport, 1954;

Much of the research reported in this chapter was supported, in part, by Grants MH-26736 from the National Institute of Mental Health and BNS-78-01211 from the National Science Foundation. The chapter was completed during the second author's term as a Fellow at the Center for Advanced Study in the Behavioral Sciences, Stanford, California. The chapter draws heavily upon previous theoretical treatments by the authors and their colleagues, especially Ross, Lepper, and Hubbard (1975), Ross (1977), Nisbett and Ross (1980), and Ross and Anderson (1980).

Katz, 1960; Taynor and Deaux, 1973) all have been shown to be extraordinarily slow to respond to new evidence. Scientists themselves have similarly been taken to task for their over-zealousness in defending pet theories against the onslaught of disconfirmed predictions, empirical anomalies, and even simple failures to replicate the studies that gave rise to those theories initially (for example, Barber, 1952; Kuhn, 1962; Mahoney, 1976, 1977).

In spite of these critiques, however, there can be no argument with the proposition that people—scientists and laypersons alike—would be ill-advised to eschew the use of preconceived theories and become unbridled empiricists. Theories, as Kurt Lewin emphasized in his famous aphorism, are too practical to give up; they structure information and events into coherent wholes, allow us to store and retrieve experiential data efficiently, and generally make our experiences more comprehensible and our behavior more adaptable. Indeed, Polanyi (1958, 1964) and others have defended an extremely conservative stance for the theory-holder in the conduct of science—a conservatism that would justify even the outright dismissal of evidence collected by reputable scientists when such evidence conflicts with a powerful and otherwise parsimonious theory and no satisfactory alternative theory has been proposed which could account for new and old evidence alike.

Inevitably, in considering the various attacks on and defenses of the human tendency to cling to existing beliefs, the questions we formulate begin to introduce concerns that are essentially normative. Do our impressions, attitudes, beliefs, and theories change as much as they *ought* to? That is, do they respond to the presentation of new data, or to the undermining of old data, as much as normative standards, or trained experts, or the consensus of reasonable and unprejudiced laypeople, or even simple common sense would dictate? The reader, we trust, recognizes from the outset that such a question is beset with barbs and snares. Very often, perhaps most of the time, there will be no straightforward normative standards to dictate exactly how much persistence or change would be warranted in a given circumstance, and neither common sense, nor an expert judge, nor a jury of one's peers can offer a confident opinion. Consider, for example, the following cases:

1. John has always believed that, while Janet, a co-worker, likes him, she has absolutely no romantic interest in him. Then, one day, she invites him to join her for a picnic lunch in the park, whereupon she begins to talk very personally, even a bit flirtatiously, about her difficulties in meeting men and adjusting to the new morality.

2. Dr. Goodman, a social worker, has always assumed that in cases of child abuse it is important to separate the child from his or her abusing parents as soon as possible. She now reads a journal article reporting that "abused children assigned to foster care homes showed significantly more evidence of social and psychological impairment, ten years after separation, than did a sample of 'matched controls' not assigned to foster care."

3. Ken, a college senior majoring in psychology, decided—on the basis of his difficulties in a course taken in his sophomore year—that he had no aptitude for statistics. In discussing this deficiency with his advisor as he con-

siders applying to graduate school, Ken is reassured: "Don't worry about that Statistics I course. With Professor Fogarty teaching it, no one possibly could understand anything. In fact, Professor Lawson, who teaches our advanced statistics seminar, took the same course from Fogarty twenty years ago, and he had even more trouble than you did."

4. Dr. Green, a clinician, long ago read about a classic study on the conditioning of neuroses and, partially on that basis, has always felt confident about the theoretical underpinnings for a particular therapeutic technique. By chance, she happens to read the original article (she previously had been exposed only to secondary sources) and, to her astonishment, she discovers major shortcomings in the design and analysis of the study.

Cases 1 and 2 involve the addition of new data that, at least superficially, seem to challenge, and hence merit some change in, the individual's prior beliefs. In cases 3 and 4 the problem involves the discrediting or "subtraction" of evidence that previously had helped give rise to a particular belief. In all four cases, *some* change in belief, or at least some reduction in confidence in that belief, clearly seems warranted. But the *amount* of change demanded is unclear. No explicit normative rules exist to guide us; and neither common sense nor a panel of evaluators could do much more than agree that "yes, *some* change in belief, or at least some attenuation of confidence in that belief, would seem to be called for."

It has been this dilemma that the present authors have wrestled with, over the last five years, in their research on belief perseverance. In this chapter we shall first review studies that investigated belief perseverance and change in contexts deliberately designed to speak to the normative issue—contexts contrived to let us specify whether subjects responded *appropriately* or *inappropriately,* either to the addition of new evidence or to the discrediting of old evidence. We shall then discuss some of the cognitive mechanisms that may underlie belief perseverance and suggest some possible procedures for overcoming them. Finally, we shall offer some general thoughts about the lay-persons inferential priorities and about the prospects for improving his or her inferential practice.

Effects of Exposure to New Evidence on Existing Theories

There can be no doubt that people assimilate the data of everyday experience to their theories, schemas, and other beliefs about the world around them. And there can be no *general* normative objection to the practice. Thus, the belief that John is a friend and Jack is an enemy, and the broader theory that our friends try to do us kindnesses and our enemies try to do us harm surely serves us well, most of the time, when we must evaluate an ambiguous action directed toward us by John or Jack. But the assimilation of data to pre-existing impressions and beliefs is normatively appropriate only if it is accompanied by the continual accommodation of such theories to the implications of the accumulation of additional data. Otherwise, the theory user runs the risk of becoming a kind of intellectual Bourbon—a person who can neither learn anything new nor forget anything old—a person whose understanding of the world cannot change even if it is erroneous, because data will be either accepted at face value, reinterpreted, or simply rejected, in a manner that practically guarantees the perseverance of pre-existing beliefs.

Does adequate theory accommodation occur in the everyday responses of the layperson? Or is the portrait of intellectual Bourbonism sketched earlier justified by a closer look at the conduct of people whose preconceived theories are confronted with relevant conflicting or disconfirmatory data? A recent experiment by Lord, Ross, and Lepper (1979) addressed precisely this issue. Two purportedly authentic studies on the deterrent effect of capital punishment were presented to subjects who had previously indicated either that they strongly believed capital punishment to be a deterrent to potential murderers, or that they strongly believed it to be no deterrent. In a counterbalanced design, subjects read first about the results and methods of a study supporting their views and then about those of a study opposing their views, or vice versa. For all subjects, one study involved a panel design, comparing murder rates for particular states before and after the introduction or elimination of the death penalty, and the other featured a concurrent design, comparing homicides in those states with and without capital punishment statutes during the same time period. For half the subjects, the panel study supported their position and the concurrent design study opposed it; for the remaining subjects the purported findings were reversed. This deliberate counterbalancing of the designs and outcomes of the studies presented to subjects permits an unusually direct examination of the relationship between data assimilation and theory accomodation. It also allows us to illustrate how normatively defensible tendencies in assimilation can lead to normatively dubious outcomes in terms of accomodation. Let us consider the three main results of exposing subjects to this mixed and contradictory data set.

First, subjects' evaluations of the quality of the two studies depended on the compatibility of their findings with subjects' own prior beliefs. Thus, subjects rated the study whose results supported their own position to be "more convincing" and "better conducted" than the study which opposed their position, regardless of the designs employed in each (Mahoney, 1977).

Second, subjects' attitudes, overall, were more influenced by exposure to results that supported their existing veiws than by exposure to results that opposed those views. Descriptions of methodological details and possible critiques of the research further enhanced these effects. Reading the details of supporting studies did little if anything to attenuate their initial impact on the subjects' attitudes; reading the details of "opposing" studies markedly reduced their already modest impact—sometimes even producing a boomerang effect, whereby the subjects' beliefs were actually *strengthened* by an opposing study, once the details of methodology and resulting possibilities for artifact and misinterpretation in that study were explicated.

The third result was an inevitable consequence of these theory-biased assimilation tendencies. Having read *both* studies, one that supported their initial position and one that opposed it, subjects became *more* polarized and confident in their views than they had been before reading any evidence. This occurred, we should note, despite the fact that the two studies were, on the average (through counterbalancing), objectively equal in their probative value.

Normatively, one would expect a pattern of mixed empirical outcomes—that is, outcomes indistinguishable from those that would have been generated, on the average, by a random number table or a coin flip—to undermine the theory-holder's confidence and to moderate the extremity of his or her views. At most, one could justify a total absence of change, if the theory-holders were so confident in their theories that data of the variety offered to them in this study were simply too weak to deserve attention. But one cannot normatively justify increased polarization, lest one justify a set of inferential biases that would guarantee that *any* theory be strengthened by any set of data offering a chance level of support.

We will have more to say about the nature and the logical status of theory-biased data assimilation a bit later in this chapter. For now, let us merely note a disturbing irony. Before the advent of modern social science, many questions, like that of the deterrent value of capital punishment, could be debated only on the basis of intuitions, dubiously relevant personal experiences, and global theories about human nature and society. One might hope, and expect, that the development of scientific techniques for the study of such issues would lead to a happier result—either to consensus, where the relevant empirical findings were consistent and conclusive, or to greater moderation and mutual tolerance by contending factions, where the evidence proved to be inconsistent and inconclusive. The findings of Lord, Ross, and Lepper, however, do little to encourage this latter hope. They suggest that mixed evidence (and the evidence is bound to be "mixed" for many pressing but complex issues of social, economic, or political policy) far from moderating public opinion, is apt to *polarize* it. Each side in a dispute is likely to accept more or less at face value any evidence that ostensibly supports their position, but to offer every possible challenge to any evidence that ostensibly supports their opponents. Certainly the history of public debate on a variety of issues in the past two decades, from the social costs and benefits of busing to the advisibility of a negative income tax or the deterrent efficacy of capital punishment itself, has been more consistent with the findings of Lord, Ross, and Lepper than with the fond hopes of social scientists.

Effects of Discrediting "Old" Evidence on Existing Theories

The second research paradigm designed to demonstrate normatively indefensible belief perseverance deals not with the addition of new evidence but with the discrediting of old evidence. As two of the cases described earlier—the student who discovers that he has been victimized by poor teaching, and the clinician who discovers flaws in a classic demonstration experiment—illustrate, it is typically difficult to specify how much readjustment of belief would be appropriate or excessive in light of a given attack on the evidential basis for that belief. There is, however, at least one case in which a decisive test is possible. That test occurs when the individual discovers that the basis for some initial impression or belief is not merely biased or tainted, but instead is completely inauthentic or invalid.

Perhaps the most obvious example occurs when subjects are debriefed after participating in an important experiment that has made use of deception. The subject is told the nature of the relevant deception and is assured that the previous information—about himself or herself, or about some peer, the experiment, or even the world outside the laboratory—was completely fictitious and can be totally disregarded. And the assumption of the experimenter is that such discrediting of previous information can eliminate whatever belief, or change in belief, was initially produced by the information.

The first of our studies (Ross, Lepper, and Hubbard, 1975) challenged this optimistic assumption directly. Subjects were recruited for a study allegedly concerned with the effects of problem-solving feedback on physiological indicators. They were then presented with a novel task—distinguishing authentic suicide notes from inauthentic ones—and, as they worked, they were given false feedback after each trial. This feedback led them to believe that they had performed, overall, at an average level, or at a level much better (success condition) or much worse (failure condition) than average. Following this manipulation of apparent outcome, subjects were thoroughly debriefed concerning the predetermined and random nature of the feedback they had received. Indeed, they were even shown the experimenter's instruction sheet, assigning to them the success, failure, or average performance condition and specifying the exact feedback to be presented. Later, subjects filled out post-experimental questionnaires requiring estimates of their "actual" performance at the task, their probable future performance, their ability at the task relative to their peers, and their ability at other related tasks.

Ross, Lepper, and Hubbard reveal that, even after a thorough debriefing, subjects continued to rate their performance and abilities in accord with the false feedback they had received. Success subjects continued to believe that they had performed well in the past, would perform well in the future, and were blessed with considerable ability at the experimental task and other tasks related to it. Failure subjects, conversely, continued to offer negative assessments of their performance and abilities.

A second experiment reported in the same paper replicated this finding and extended it, as well, to the domain of social perceptions. Observers, who merely witnessed the actors' performance and the relevant initial feedback and subsequent debriefing, proved just as inclined to persevere in their initial impressions about the actors as were the actors themselves. In fact, comparisons of debriefed subjects with nondebriefed controls indicated that only about half of the initial impact of the false feedback was eliminated—for either actors or observers—through a standard, thorough debriefing procedure.

Demonstrations of post-debriefing belief perseverance have now been extended to a variety of impressions (Fleming and Arrowood, in press; Jennings, Lepper, and Ross, 1980; Sagotsky, Lazinski, and Konop, 1979;

Valins, 1974; Walster and others, 1967), and even relatively abstract theories (Anderson, Lepper, and Ross, in press). Comparable results appear, as well, across a variety of debriefing or discrediting procedures (Jennings and others, 1980; Sagotsky and others, 1979).

Two experiments conducted outside the laboratory setting by Lepper, Ross, and Lau (1980) offer a particularly clear demonstration that such perseverance phenomena are more than hot-house products of carefully contrived laboratory methodology. In these studies, students at a local high school were first led to form erroneous impressions of their ability to solve logical reasoning problems (problems in which various clues can be used to match a set of actors with a specified set of occupations, hobbies, preferences, and so on). This was accompanied by varying the quality of instruction given to the students. Half received a clear coherent lecture that promoted subsequent success by illustrating the use of a simple matrix to solve one of the seemingly difficult and complex puzzles. The remaining subjects, by contrast, witnessed the solution of the same puzzle accompanied by a rambling, confusing, and generally unhelpful series of exhortations. All of the subjects then attempted to solve a series of puzzles on their own. As planned, the effectively tutored or success-condition subjects performed well at the task, while the failure-condition subjects performed poorly.

Following these instructional sessions and tests, half of the subjects in each condition were fully debriefed on the likely cause of their test performance. In fact, in one of these studies subjects actually viewed the videotaped lecture that previously had been shown to subjects in the opposite condition, and were able to solve the sample problem, along with the instructor, using this second technique. The remaining subjects were exposed to no such debriefing procedure. All participants then rated their abilities at the task, their liking for it, and their probable future performance at it and related tasks. In addition, they were asked directly to estimate the impact of the two teaching performances. Finally, in a subsequent situation dissociated from the experimental setting, a delayed posttest was administered. Students were asked, in their regular classrooms, to respond to a survey allegedly conducted by the school's mathematics department. This survey solicited the students' reactions to various potential additions to the department's curriculum, including one featuring the same sort of problem-solving tasks presented in the experimental sessions several weeks before.

The findings of Lepper, Ross, and Lau provide a striking demonstration that self-assessments, once formed, can survive the most pointed attacks on their origins. Even though subjects knew that they initially had been the victim (or beneficiary) of inferior (or superior) teaching; even though they could accurately predict the differential performance levels that would result from the two teaching techniques; indeed, even when the initial damage done to one group was effectively undone with exposure to the superior teaching techniques, the differences between the groups persisted. Particularly dramatic were findings on the delayed follow-up measures. Not only were the "debriefed" subjects' self-appraisals still influenced by their initial experiences, these subjects were virtually indistinguishable on most of the measures from the subjects who had never been debriefed at all.

Mechanisms Promoting Belief Perseverance

The research cited thus far, and a wealth of everyday experience, indicates that beliefs can survive potent logical or empirical challenges (Abelson, 1959). Beliefs can survive, and even be bolstered by, evidence that uncommitted observers would agree logically demands some weakening of them. They can even survive the total destruction of their original evidential basis. Much work remains to be done in specifying the precise limits of and possible exceptions to the perseverance phenomenon (Hatvany and Strack, in press), but the phenomenon itself seems genuine. The questions that arise, therefore, are *how* and *why* does belief perseverance occur?

One obvious answer is that people sometimes persevere in their beliefs for motivational reasons—because those beliefs embody strongly held values (Rokeach, 1973), because they serve some function for the individual (Katz, 1960), or because they are buttressed by behavioral commitments or whole networks of related, consonant attitudes and cognitions (Festinger, 1957; Heider, 1958; Osgood and Tannenbaum, 1955; Rosenberg, 1960). No doubt motivational, emotional, or behavioral commitments often play a role in the perseverance of beliefs. However, such commitments seem to provide neither a sufficient explanation of nor a necessary condition for belief perseverance.

Even when the individual is motivated to maintain a given belief, there generally must be some cognitive mechanisms that allow him or her to accomplish this goal (Abelson, 1959; Allport, 1954). People do occasionally say, "my mind's made up, don't bother me with the facts"; but more typically, they are prepared to maintain that their beliefs are congruent with, if not demanded by, the best evidence available. The question of underlying mechanisms thus remains: What cognitive processes protect existing beliefs from the impact of logical or empirical attacks that seem, normatively, irresistible?

Conversely, it also seems clear that belief perseverance can occur in the absence of any apparent motivational or behavioral commitment. Is it not hard to imagine, for example, that subjects in the failure conditions of the Ross, Lepper, and Hubbard studies were motivated to persevere in the belief that they were unusually inept at discriminating genuine suicide notes from fakes? Nor is it clear what motive observers in these same studies have to maintain their initially positive or negative impressions of the actor. Indeed, the case against a purely motivational interpretation of these effects can be made somewhat more forcefully. In the Ross and others (1977) studies, for example, there is no indication that the perseverant effects of apparent initial failure are even less powerful than those of initial success. Nor do such effects appear to depend on, or vary with, either chronic or acute differences in subjects' level of concern regarding the abilities in question (Walster and others, 1967). Hence some nonmotivational mechanisms appear implicated.

Biased Search, Recollection, and Assimilation of Evidence. Perhaps the most obvious class of perseverance mechanisms arises from the role that existing beliefs and expectations play whenever one processes information. The events we witness, the reports other provide us, indeed new data that we receive from any source, are processed in the light of our preconceptions. The result is a bias that tends to offer confirmation of those preconceptions and the broader theories that underlie them.

Beyond the inevitable encoding and decoding biases that make our spontaneous observations and recollections appear to confirm our expectancies (see Hamilton, 1979; Hastie and Kumar, 1979), there is also evidence that confirming cases are both more likely to be searched for, and more likely to be regarded as relevant, when one engages in deliberate hypothesis testing (Snyder and Swann, 1978b). This generalization holds, moreover, even when the hypothesis or theory under consideration is not one to which the individual is in any way committed (Wason and Johnson-Laird, 1965).

Most important of all, perhaps, is the theory-holder's response to equivocal data—that is, evidence inherently ambiguous or of questionable reliability, validity, or relevance. Once again, our preconceptions will guide the weighting and interpretation of such data, resulting in a further inevitable confirmation bias. For example, when one sees or hears of an incident in which a priest pats a small child on the head, enters a church, or speaks of the rewards of celibacy and self-denial, one accepts the event at face value and one's entire network of beliefs about priests is thereby strengthened. But let the incident be one in which the priest throws stones at a small child or holds forth on the joys of free love and self-indulgence, and one's response to the datum will no longer be uncritical acceptance. Alternative explanations will spring to the fore ("It wasn't a priest—it must have been someone just dressed up like one") or reinterpretations will be considered that somehow render the datum less hostile to one's existing beliefs ("It wasn't a *'real'* priest; it must have been one of those radical revisionists whom the church is trying to expel" or "The poor priest couldn't have been himself; he must have been in the throes of a mental breakdown").

Two consequences follow from such theory-biased responses to evidence. First, virtually any pattern of evidence processed in this fashion, even evidence that is essentially random, will tend to *bolster* one's initial belief (see Chapman and Chapman, 1967, 1969). Second, once evidence has been processed in this fashion, it gains the capacity to *sustain* the prior belief when that belief is subjected to new empirical disconfirmations or to attacks on its original evidential bases. In a sense, the person will have the illusion that his or her theory enjoys many *independent* sources of support, each of which is sufficient, but not necessary, for its maintenance.

The Lord, Lepper, and Ross findings, cited earlier, offered some fairly direct evidence for the operation of these biased assimilation mechanisms in the new information paradigm. Their operation in the discounting or debriefing paradigm, however, is somewhat less obvious and more speculative. We suggest that the subject who forms an initial impression about himself, about another person, or about some functional relationship in the environment, is apt to search his memory and the immediate situation for *additional* data relevant to that impression. Such data, however, are apt to be recalled, and regarded as pertinent or probative, only to the extent that they confirm the impression at hand. Thus a subject who has succeeded or failed at a given task may recall previous successes or failures at related tasks—the decision about the relevance of any such prior task outcome to the present case, however, will importantly depend upon its congruence with one's present outcome. Similarly, a subject who has come to believe that variables X and Y are functionally related will recall, and give credence to, cases that confirm rather than challenge that presumed relationship.

Not only may such biased search, recollection, and assimilation processes bolster one's initial beliefs; they may also produce a pattern of biased evidence that remains highly available to sustain the belief in question even when the initial basis for that belief has been attacked or eliminated. In a sense, the critical assumption here is that the individual does not constantly, or fully, update and reevaluate the evidence relevant to his or her beliefs. Although the individual may accept a particularly compelling refutation of specific findings or outcomes that initially led to a particular belief or hypothesis, he or she is unlikely to take the further step of deciding, "now that my hypothesis has been partially undermined, I must go back and reassess *all* of the evidence that I considered in light of that hypothesis."

Before proceeding to discuss additional mechanisms underlying belief perseverance, let us pause to make a couple of obvious, but important, points about the normative status of biased data assimilation. First, it is obvious that the theory-holder is well served, most of the time, by this bias. Undoubtedly, it promotes more cases of accurate interpretations than error. (Priests who act in priestly fashion generally are what they seem to be, and people who look like priests but act in ways that violate our strongest and most basic assumptions about priests very well may *not* be what they seem to be.) Moreover, any purer empiricism, even if it were possible, and even if it were apt to lead to fewer errors, surely would rarely justify the tremendous additional demands it would make on our information-processing capacities. Nevertheless, there may be specific situations or inferential domains in which the costs of theory-biased processing are unacceptable, and in which possible remedies are both feasible and desirable. These issues will be addressed further in the concluding section of this chapter.

The Formation of Causal Explanations and Scenarios. A second, related mechanism promoting belief perseverance is somewhat less obvious and familiar, but derives (Ross, Lepper, and Hubbard, 1975) from the basic assumption that individuals do more than merely note evidence and assess its congruence with current impressions or beliefs. People try to *account* for the state of affairs that is captured in their beliefs (Kelley, 1967). Thus the subject who suddenly finds herself confronted with evidence of her superior or inferior ability at discriminating suicide notes might search for some aspect of her background or personality that might account for such a talent or deficiency. The seemingly successful subject, for example, may credit her performance to her familiarity with the self-revealing poetry of an author who later committed suicide; the apparent failure may cite her own cheerful and optimistic disposition as an impediment to the empathetic set the task demands.

Once again this mechanism both bolsters existing beliefs and sustains them in the face of subsequent challenges. The subject who has explained an initial superior or inferior performance at a given task is not going to be overly influenced by the later revelation that this original task outcome was contrived by the experimenter ("Even if I don't have any authentic feedback about how well I did in that little test before, I'm sure I did well and that I'm good at that kind of thing—after all, I have all these keen insights about the mind of the potential suicide that are bound to help me"). What such a subject fails to recognize, we contend, is that it was only the task of accounting for an unexpected degree of success that made familiarity with a writer who committed suicide become salient and seemingly relevant to predicting performance at this task.

Direct evidence for the operation of this causal explanation mechanism comes from several sources. Anderson, Lepper, and Ross (in press), for example, report two debriefing studies that demonstrate that the magnitude of the perseverance of social theories can be enhanced by explicitly requiring subjects to formulate such explanations prior to debriefing. In these studies, subjects were first led to believe that either a positive or a negative relationship existed between two measured variables—the adequacy of firefighters' on-the-job performance and their prior scores on a paper-and-pencil test of risk preference. Interestingly, this initial belief could be manipulated by providing evidence about a single pair of concrete cases—one successful firefighter and one unsuccessful one, with appropriately discrepant risk-taking scores. Before debriefing, some subjects were simply asked to provide an explanation of the relationship observed in the two case studies. Not surprisingly, they had little difficulty in generating such explanations ("You have to be brave enough to take risks, or you'll never succeed in a job like firefighting" or, alternatively "Foolhardy individuals who take a lot of risks are bound to get into trouble in a dangerous job like firefighting"). Furthermore, these explanation subjects proved particularly reluctant to change their minds when they found out that the formative evidence for their theory was invalid; their estimates of the true relationship between the two variables were virtually indistinguishable from those made by subjects who had never been debriefed at all!

Similar effects have also been observed in the domains of self and social perceptions. Fleming and Arrowood (in press) placed subjects in the Ross, Lepper, and Hubbard (1975) "suicide note" paradigm, and examined the effects of procedures designed either to induce subjects to provide an explicit explanation of their purported initial success or failure or to distract them from considering the causes of their initial performance. Relative to a replication condition given no specific instructions, interpolation of an explanation task before debriefing increased belief perseverance whereas interpolation of a distraction task decreased belief perseverance. Likewise, in a social-perception paradigm, Ross and others (1977) have shown that subjects who explain outcomes (such as a hit-and-run car accident) in the lives of clinical patients whose case histories they have previously read, continue to regard such outcomes as relatively likely even after learning that the explained events were inauthentic and had been contrived by the experimenter.

The same mechanism enhancing subjective likelihood, incidentally, apparently operates outside the debriefing paradigm. Other subjects in the Ross and others (1977) studies were asked to provide explanations for clinical outcomes knowing from the outset that the outcomes were merely hypothetical. Nevertheless, once an event had been explained—related to antecedent events that could have caused it, or at least foreshadowed it—the event seemed more likely to occur. Fischhoff's (1975, 1976; Fischhoff and Beyth, 1975) "certainty of hindsight" phenomenon may also depend on the same mechanism; events that did occur are related to known causal antecedents and, once those causal links have become salient and available, the consequent historical event seems to have been both inevitable and predictable from the information available to contemporary observers.

As in the case of biased assimilation, the operation of this causal explanation mechanism in producing belief perseverance and hindsight certainty raises subtle normative issues. Essentially, subjects showed themselves willing to believe that events (or relationships between variables) were probable to the extent that they could readily be derived from some causal model or theory. There is nothing logically or normatively wrong with the use of such a criterion. Certainly, any formal scientist would be well-advised to do likewise when a theoretically-derived hypothesis fails to be confirmed in a given experimental test. The problem arises only when flimsy, ad hoc theories are invented for the purpose at hand, and causal mechanisms that would have predicted other events or relationships are both initially overlooked and never reconsidered when the individual's initial presumptions are discredited or challenged by new data. In a sense the problem is more metacognitive than normative. Subjects appear to underestimate the ease with which virtually *any* outcomes, even mutually contradictory one, can adequately be explained. They underestimate their own fecundity as causal theorists, and hence are overly convinced of the veridicality of their beliefs by the ease with which they were able to postulate relevant causal linkages.

Behavioral Confirmation Biases. While the experiments cited thus far capture many of the elements of everyday belief perseverance, they lack one element that may be the most critical of all—they deny subjects the opportunity to *act* on their beliefs. The fact that people do act on their beliefs is important in everyday contexts, in part, because behavioral commitment increases the psychological costs or dissonance involved in altering one's beliefs (Collins and Hoyt, 1972; Festinger, 1957; Wicklund and Brehm, 1976). This presumably should increase the tendency to bias one's search for and interpretation of evi dence. But the opportunity for action also creates the possibility that the data themselves will be biased in a manner that serves to support the actor's hypothesis or belief—the possibility that our prophecies may prove self-fulfilling (Jones, 1977; Merton, 1948).

Rosenthal and Jacobson's (1968) famous "Pygmalion" studies, for example, demonstrated that teachers' expectations concerning the abilities of their pupils could influence the performance of students in a manner that led to the apparent confirmation of those expectations. Although these initial findings have proved a source of some controversy, it is clear that expectancy effects of this sort do occur (Jones, 1977; Rosenthal, 1976). More recent research, for example, illustrates more precisely how specific, and initially erroneous, impressions or beliefs about others can lead to reciprocated social reactions that offer objective support for those beliefs. In one particularly elegant set of demonstrations, Snyder and his colleagues (Snyder and Swann, 1978a; Snyder, Tanke, and Berscheid, 1977) have traced the complete chain of events through which differential initial expectations concerning the appearance or personality of another are translated into differences in behavior toward that other person that, in turn, produce significant differences in the responses *of* that other person consistent with the perceiver's initial expectancies.

Anecdotal evidence for this mechanism, we suspect, is also familiar to our readers. The young woman who accepts sexist theories about the aptitudes, and accordingly chooses or avoids academic and social experiences in a manner that makes such theories accurate, is one case in point. The suitor or job candidate who believes he will be rejected, and then acts so unconfidently that he *is* rejected, is another (see Nisbett and Ross, 1980, for further discussion).

What normative objection can be raised here? Should people not act on their impressions and beliefs? Should they disregard the evidence that arises as a direct or indirect consequence of their own actions? Or should they merely be aware of, and somehow make allowance for, the problem? We soon shall have more to say about this and other normative issues. But first, let us pause to consider the fact that, perseverance mechanisms notwithstanding, impressions, theories, and other beliefs *do* sometimes change.

When Beliefs Yield to Evidence

None of us holds exactly the same view of ourself, our peers, or our society that we once did. Children eventually renounce their faith in Santa Claus; once popular political leaders fall into disrepute, and a generation of feminists has somehow managed to overturn popular views about women and sex roles. Even scientists sometimes change their views!

Clearly, the occurrence of such changes in attitudes and beliefs poses no fundamental contradiction to the thesis advanced in this chapter. No one, certainly not the present authors, has ever denied that new evidence or attacks on old evidence can produce change. Our contention is simply that such changes generally will occur more slowly, and less markedly, than would be normatively justified—that more, or more compelling, evidence will often be required to alter an initial belief than to create it (Hovland, 1959).

At the same time, it is also clear that the mechanisms underlying belief perseverance can sometimes be overcome without massive doses of logically compelling evidence or argumentation. Dramatic religious and political conversions, for example, are rarely accomplished by painstaking attacks on individual beliefs or the dispassionate presentation of masses of new data. More typically, the prospective convert is induced to reject entire networks of beliefs, and is pressured to adopt a new, and highly biased, alternative belief system for interpreting relevant evidence (Frank, 1961). Insight therapies similarly attempt to overcome resistent beliefs through a combination of global assaults on the individual's current, dysfunctional belief system and the introduction of new explanatory or inferential schemas. Comparable processes, through which older theories may be supplanted by new and often incommensurate paradigms, have been suggested by Kuhn (1962) to underlie major advances in formal science. Such revolutions in our beliefs, value systems, or scientific formulations all seem to depend upon a central set of ingredients: latent dissatisfaction with existing belief systems occasioned by the existence of disconfirming or anomalous evidence, external pressures to change, and the availability of a satisfactory alternative model that accounts for old and new data alike.

In this regard, one further finding of the Ross, Lepper, and Hubbard (1975) suicide note study merits particular attention. In our previous discussion of these studies, we have focussed on the relative ineffectiveness of standard outcome debriefing procedures—in which subjects were simply made aware that the feedback they had received, indicating their apparent success or failure, was inauthentic and preprogrammed—in eliminating subject's initial, ill-founded beliefs about their abilities. These studies also included, however, a set of process debriefing conditions—in which subjects were given, in addition, some insight and concrete illustrations regarding the nature of the assimilation and explanation mechanisms that might prompt belief perseverance and were encouraged not to fall prey to these biases. Belief perseverance, under these conditions, was almost wholly eliminated.

Finally, we should note that the same factors that contribute to an item of information's initial impact on our beliefs may also determine its capacity to overcome existing impressions, beliefs, or theories (Nisbett and Ross, 1980). Thus it is information that is valid, concrete, based on first-hand experience, and easily assimilated to pre-existing knowledge schemas, that is most apt to overcome initial beliefs. Indeed, such information may even be able to eliminate initial beliefs that are well founded and correct. Although a great deal of research has been done addressing the issue of when and why beliefs yield to evidence (see Kiesler, Collins, and Miller, 1969; McGuire, 1966), it is worth noting that the normative issue has been all but ignored in such research. We know a great deal about the kinds of communicators, messages, audiences, and settings that are conducive to attitude change, yet this research provides us with little insight about the appropriateness of the changes produced by these factors or the adaptiveness of the processes that mediate such changes.

Some Implications and Conclusions

We have argued in this chapter that normatively unjustifiable belief perseverance occurs as the more or less inevitable consequence of certain cognitive mechanisms, each of which itself raises subtle normative issues. We have by no means exhausted these normative issues (see Sklar, 1975), but we have wrestled with them enough to justify the following conclusion: Overall, the mechanisms that produce belief perseverance—that is, theory-biased processing of evidence, the tendency to formulate causal explanations, and the willingness to act on one's beliefs—undoubtedly do the individual more good than harm. In a sense, belief perseverance is a local cost of generally cost-efficient cognitive and behavioral strategies. Let us turn, then, to a further consideration of these costs and procedures for promoting appropriate accommodation of beliefs and theories to further data.

Accuracy and Other Superordinate Goals in Information-Processing. At several points in this chapter we have emphasized that the willingness to let one's theory-based preconceptions bias the processing of information—particularly information that is ambiguous or of uncertain validity—undoubtedly serves the goal of overall accuracy, even if it may produce errors in many individual cases. We now will try to explicate and qualify this contention. Before doing so, however, we should emphasize that a heavy reliance upon preconceptions may also serve epistemic goals other than, and often superordinate to, sheer accuracy (Goldman, 1978; Nisbett and Ross, 1980).

Two such superordinate goals are: (1) the importance of coherence and stability in one's belief system, even at the cost of occasional logical or empirical inconsistencies, and (2) the real-world constraints on processing time and capacity that both preclude the careful, dispassionate, perusal of evidence and reward any strategy that frees such time and capacity for other more cost effective endeavors. That is, a *general* belief conservatism and willingness to wear theoretical blinders may be rewarded by intellectual and emotional gains that more than compensate for occasional, domain-specific errors in interpreting the world. Moreover, in those specific cases where one's preconceptions are *seriously* wrong, so that everyday experience produces masses of relevant data that decisively contradict those preconceptions, change will occur.

Even if we were to consider only the accuracy issue, however, simple generalizations about normativeness or counternormativeness are apt to be misleading. Obviously, not all theories are equal in their utility or validity. Accordingly, the normativeness of conserving particular theories or employing them heavily in data collection and interpretation depends upon their logical and empirical status. The theory that Joan is shy (arrived at because she said "no thanks" last week when you offered to introduce her to the guests at a party) is not as well founded, nor apt to be as useful in future data interpretation, as the theory that Joan is a college professor (arrived at because she told you so). Accordingly, the normativeness of interpreting subsequent ambiguous behavior as "professional" is greater, all things being equal, than the normativeness of interpreting subsequent ambiguous behavior as shy. By the same token, the normativeness of seeking alternative interpretations for actions or outcomes inconsistent with the role of professor is greater than the normativeness of seeking alternative explanations for behavior that seems inconsistent with shyness. On the same grounds, it is less legitimate to code a patient's ambiguous remark on the basis of psychoanalytic theory than it is to code an ambiguous measurement of time or distance on the basis of some axiom of Newtonian physics.

Ultimately, our point becomes a truism: that one is better served by good and powerful theories than by poor or weak ones. But the truism has some important implications. One implication is that when dealing with a domain in which one's preconceptions, impressions, and theories rest on flimsy inferential grounds and are relatively untested, one should become less theory-driven and more data-driven in one's judgments. One should try to retain raw data in as pure a form as possible, to avoid early theorizing, and to engage in frequent reassessment of all the available data. Impressions about people, particularly broad dispositional inferences based on highly situation-specific responses, constitute one such domain where the early formulation and employment of theories is not a cost efficient inferential strategy. A second implication is the need for monitoring one's inferential conduct. Specifically, when one finds that one is being forced to do a lot of reinterpretation of data because some particular theory-based preconception is frequently being disconfirmed, one ought to reconsider carefully whether the logical and empirical basis for that theory, and/or the leap from it to one's particular preconception, is solid enough to justify such heroic efforts.

Techniques for Accommodating Beliefs to Data. Given the various mechanisms that make theories appear to enjoy more objective and independent sources of support than is actually the case, what options exist for the intuitive scientist who wishes to test those theories in a more even-handed manner? At least one avenue of redress seems obvious. One can seek to eliminate the relevant biases, or compensate for them, by trying to appreciate how the world looks through the eyes of an individual who holds alternative beliefs. (If pure imagination or role-playing fails, such individuals will often be quite willing to tell us how the world looks to them, if only we will listen). One can reconsider formative evidence, or try to recall additional evidence from this opposing theoretical perspective; one can formulate explanations for alternative states of affairs or alternative functional relationships; one can even speculate, and collect evidence, about how the available data might look if one had acted on the basis of rival beliefs. One can further try to make certain that any new evidence, or any challenge to old evidence, is presented in a fashion that is as vivid, concrete, and personally relevant as the evidence that originally occasioned such beliefs (see Nisbet and Ross, 1980).

Having offered such advice, however, the authors are left uneasy. For it may well be too vague, and too unrealistic in terms of its cognitive demands, to be of practical value in most inferential contexts. Two alternatives, accordingly, will be proposed.

First, one can accept the fact that the informally available data relevant to one's existing impressions and beliefs are inevitably biased, and therefore try to make appropriate adjustments in one's decision criteria. Rather than attempting to purify the available data, one can simply shift one's criteria in judging the status of one's hypothesis in a manner analogous to the way one compensates for a violation of the assumptions underlying a given statistical test. The question thus becomes not "is my hypothesis generally supported by the available evidence," but rather "is my hypothesis supported as strongly as one might expect in light of the powerful mechanisms that are biasing the data in its favor?" While more precise inferential guides cannot yet be formulated, it is at least clear that one might adjust upward one's criteria for confirmation whenever one is dealing with inherently ambiguous or inconclusive data, or a theory that is difficult to refute because it offers few unequivocal and testable predictions.

Finally, one can resort to the time-honored method of the scientist by substituting relatively formal theory-testing procedures for informal or intuitive ones. Often, by holding some factors constant and systematically manipulating others, one can decisively reject erroneous beliefs, even ones that hold great intuitive appeal. Full-blown experiments are rarely feasible in testing the informal and often poorly defined beliefs pertinent to everyday experience. Nevertheless, it is surprising how seldom we even try to approximate them in our ordinary affairs. The parent who believes that his or her child's nightmares are the product of television programs rarely runs the controlled experiment of randomly designating TV and non-TV days and noting the nocturnal consequences. The merchant who believes that "loss-leaders" are good or bad for business is far less likely to speculate about the relevant policy than to manipulate it and thereby gain valid information vitally important to the conduct of his business (Doob and others, 1969).

The foregoing testimonial for the scientific method in general, and for controlled experiments in particular, should not be misunderstood. We know all too well that the scientific method is not immune to the diseases of biased assimilation, causal explanation, and a host of other nagging afflictions; scientists can be blind, sometimes deliberately so, to unanticipated or uncongenial interpretations of their data and recalcitrant in their theoretical allegiances (Kuhn, 1962; Mahoney, 1976, 1977). Nevertheless, it is the scientific method—with its gradual substitution first of data for conjecture, and then of well-controlled, carefully focused experiments for naturalistic observation—that has often been responsible for increasing human understanding of the natural and social world. Despite its flaws, it remains the best means of delivering us from the errors of intuitive beliefs and intuitive methods for testing those beliefs.

As Bacon put the case for an experimental method three and a half centuries ago:

> Not only is a greater abundance of experiments to be sought for and procured, and that too of a different kind from those hitherto tried; an entirely different method, order, and process for carrying on and advancing experience must also be introduced. For experience when it wanders in its own track, is, as I have already remarked, mere groping in the dark, and confounds men rather than instructs them. But when it shall proceed in accordance with a fixed law, in regular order, and without interruption, then may better things be hoped of knowledge (1960 [1620], p. 96).

References

Abelson, R. P. "Modes of Resolution of Belief Dilemmas." *Conflict Resolution,* 1959, *3,* 343-352.
Allport, G. W. *The Nature of Prejudice.* Reading, Mass.: Addison-Wesley, 1954.
Anderson, C. A., Lepper, M. R., and Ross, L. "The Perseverance of Social Theories: The Role of Explanation in the Persistence of Discredited Information." *Journal of Personality and Social Psychology,* in press.
Asch, S. "Forming Impressions of Personality." *Journal of Abnormal and Social Psychology,* 1946, *41,* 258-290.
Bacon, F. *The New Organon and Related Writings.* New York: Liberal Arts Press, 1960. (Originally published 1620.)
Barber, B. *Science and the Social Order.* New York: Collier, 1952.
Chapman, L., and Chapman, J. "The Genesis of Popular but Erroneous Psychodiagnostic Observations." *Journal of Abnormal Psychology,* 1967, *72,* 193-204.
Chapman, L., and Chapman, J. "Illusory Correlation as an Obstacle to the Use of Valid Psychodiagnostic Signs." *Journal of Abnormal Psychology,* 1969, *74,* 271-280.
Collins, B. E., and Hoyt, M. F. "Personal Responsibility-for-Consequences: An Integration and Extension of the Forced-Compliance Literature." *Journal of Experimental Social Psychology,* 1972, *8,* 558-593.
Doob, A. N., Carlsmith, J. M., Freedman, J. L., Landauer, T. K., and Tom, S., Jr. "Effect of Initial Selling Price on Subsequent Sales." *Journal of Personality and Social Psychology,* 1969, *11,* 345-350.
Festinger, L. *A Theory of Cognitive Dissonance.* Stanford, Calif.: Stanford University Press, 1957.
Fischhoff, B. "Hindsight ≠ Foresight: The Effect of Outcome Knowledge on Judgment Under Uncertainty." *Journal of Experimental Psychology: Human Perception and Performance,* 1975, *1,* 288-299.
Fischhoff, B. "Attribution Theory and Judgment Under Uncertainty." In J. Harvey, W. Ickes, and R. Kidd (Eds.), *New Directions in Attribution Research,* Vol. 1. Hillsdale, N.J.: Erlbaum, 1976.
Fischhoff, B., and Beyth, R. "'I Knew It Would Happen'—Remembered Probabilities of Once-Future Things." *Organizational Behavior and Human Performance,* 1975, *13,* 1-16.
Fleming, J., and Arrowood, A. J. "Information Processing and the Perseverance of Discredited Self-Perceptions." *Personality and Social Psychology Bulletin,* in press.
Frank, J. D. *Persuasion and Healing.* Baltimore, Md.: The Johns Hopkins University Press, 1961.
Goldman, A. I. "Epistemics: The Regulative Theory of Cognition." *The Journal of Philosophy,* 1978, *75,* 509-524.
Hamilton, D. L. "A Cognitive Attributional Analysis of Sterotyping." In L. Berkowitz (Ed.), *Advances in Experimental Social Psychology.* Vol. 12. New York: Academic Press, 1979.
Hastie, R., and Kumar, P. A. "Person Memory: Personality Traits as Organizing Principles in Memory for Behavior." *Journal of Personality and Social Psychology,* 1979, *37,* 25-38.
Hatvany, N., and Strack, F. "The Impact of a Discredited Key Witness." *Journal of Applied Social Psychology,* in press.
Heider, F. *The Psychology of Interpersonal Relations.* New York: Wiley, 1958.
Hovland, C. I. "Reconciling Results Derived from Experimental and Survey Studies of Attitude Change." *American Psychologist,* 1959, *14,* 8-17.
Janis, I. L. "Stages in the Decision-Making Process." In R. P. Abelson, E. Aronson, W. J. McGuire, T. M. Newcomb, M. J. Rosenberg, and P. H. Tannenbaum (Eds.), *Theories of Cognitive Consistency: A Sourcebook.* Chicago: Rand McNally, 1968.

Jennings, D. L., Lepper, M. R., and Ross, L. "Persistence of Impressions of Personal Persuasiveness." Unpublished manuscript, Stanford University, 1980.
Jones, E. E., and Goethals, G. R. "Order Effects in Impression Formation: Attribution Context and the Nature of the Entity." In E. E. Jones and others (Eds.), *Attribution: Perceiving the Causes of Behavior.* Morristown, N.J.: General Learning Press, 1971.
Jones, R. A. *Self-Fulfilling Prophecies.* Hillsdale, N.J.: Erlbaum, 1977.
Katz, D. "The Functional Approach to the Study of Attitudes." *Public Opinion Quarterly,* 1960, *24,* 163-204.
Kelley, H. H. "Attribution Theory in Social Psychology." In D. Levine (Ed.), *Nebraska Symposium on Motivation.* Vol. 15. Lincoln: University of Nebraska Press, 1967.
Kiesler, C. A., Collins, B. E., and Miller, N. *Attitude Change: A Critical Analysis of Theoretical Approaches.* New York: Wiley, 1969.
Kuhn, T. S. *The Structure of Scientific Revolutions.* Chicago: University of Chicago Press, 1962.
Lepper, M. R., Ross, L., and Lau, R. R. "Persistence of Inaccurate and Discredited Personal Impressions: Field Demonstrations of Attributional Perseverance in Educational Contexts." Unpublished manuscript, Stanford University, 1980.
Lord, C., Ross, L., and Lepper, M. R. "Biased Assimilation and Attitude Polarization: The Effects of Prior Theories on Subsequently Considered Evidence." *Journal of Personality and Social Psychology,* 1979, *37,* 2098-2109.
Luchins, A. S. "Mechanization in Problem Solving: The Effect of Einstellung." *Psychological Monographs,* 1942, *54,* 1-95.
Luchins, A. S. "Experimental Attempts to Minimize the Impact of First Impressions." In C. I. Hovland and others (Eds.), *The Order of Presentation in Persuasion.* New Haven, Conn.: Yale University Press, 1957.
McGuire, W. J. "Attitudes and Opinions." *Annual Review of Psychology,* 1966, *17,* 475-514.
Mahoney, M. J. *Scientist as Subject: The Psychological Imperative.* Cambridge, Mass.: Ballinger, 1976.
Mahoney, M. J. "Publication Prejudices: An Experimental Study of Confirmatory Biases in the Peer Review System." *Cognitive Therapy and Research,* 1977, *1,* 161-175.
Massad, C. M., Hubbard, M., and Newtson, D. "Selective Perception of Events." *Journal of Experimental Social Psychology,* 1979, *15,* 513-532.
Merton, R. K. "The Self-Fulfilling Prophecy." *Antioch Review,* 1948, *8,* 193-210.
Nisbett, R. E., and Ross, L. *Human Inference: Strategies and Shortcomings of Social Judgment.* Englewood Cliffs, N.J.: Prentice-Hall, 1980.
Osgood, C. E., and Tannenbaum, P. H. "The Principle of Congruity in the Prediction of Attitude Change." *Psychology Review,* 1955, *62,* 42-55.
Polyani, M. *Personal Knowledge: Towards a Post-Critical Philosophy.* New York: Harper & Row, 1958.
Polyani, M. *Science, Faith, and Society.* Chicago: University of Chicago Press, 1964.
Rokeach, M. *The Nature of Human Values.* New York: The Free Press, 1973.
Rosenberg, M. J. "Cognitive Reorganization in Response to the Hypnotic Reversal of Attitudinal Affect." *Journal of Personality,* 1960, *28,* 39-63.
Rosenthal, R. *Experimenter Effects in Behavioral Research.* New York: Irvington, 1976.
Rosenthal, R., and Jacobson, L. *Pygmalion in the Classroom: Teacher Expectation and Pupils' Intellectual Development.* New York: Holt, Rinehart and Winston, 1968.
Ross, L. "The Intuitive Psychologist and His Shortcomings." In L. Berkowitz (Ed.), *Advances in Experimental Social Psychology.* Vol. 10. New York: Academic Press, 1977.
Ross, L., and Anderson, C. "Shortcomings in the Attribution Process: On the Origins and Maintenance of Erroneous Social Assessments." In A. Tversky, D. Kahneman, and P. Slovic (Eds.), *Judgment Under Uncertainty: Heuristics and Biases.* New York: Cambridge University Press, 1980.
Ross, L., Lepper, M. R., and Hubbard, M. "Perseverance in Self-Perception and

Social Perception: Biased Attributional Processes in the Debriefing Paradigm." *Journal of Personality and Social Psychology,* 1975, *32,* 880–892.

Ross, L., Lepper, M. R., Strack, F., and Steinmetz, J. L. "Social Explanation and Social Expectation: The Effects of Real and Hypothetical Explanations Upon Subjective Likelihood." *Journal of Personality and Social Psychology,* 1977, *35,* 817–829.

Sagotsky, G., Lazinski, B., and Konop, M. "Would You Believe a Broken Computer? A Test of the Attributional Perseverance Hypothesis." Unpublished manuscript, Adelphi University, 1979.

Sklar, L. "Methodological Conservativism." *Philosophical Review,* 1975, *84,* 374–399.

Snyder, M., and Swann, W. B., Jr. "Behavioral Confirmation in Social Interaction: From Social Perception to Social Reality." *Journal of Experimental Social Psychology,* 1978a, *14,* 148–162.

Snyder, M., and Swann, W. B., Jr. "Hypothesis-Testing Processes in Social Interaction." *Journal of Personality and Social Psychology,* 1978b, *36,* 1202–1212.

Snyder, M., Tanke, E. D., and Bersheid, E. "Social Perception and Interpersonal Behavior: On the Self-Fulfilling Nature of Social Stereotypes." *Journal of Personality and Social Psychology,* 1977, *5,* 656–666.

Taynor, J., and Deaux, K. "When Women Are More Deserving Than Men: Equity, Attribution, and Perceived Sex Differences." *Journal of Personality and Social Psychology,* 1973, *28,* 360–367.

Valins, S. "Persistent Effects of Information About Internal Reactions: Ineffectiveness of Debriefing." In H. London and R. E. Nisbett (Eds.), *Thought and Feeling: Cognitive Modification of Feeling States.* Chicago: Aldine, 1974.

Walster, E., Berscheid, E., Abrahams, D., and Aronson, V. "Effectiveness of Debriefing Following Deception Experiments." *Journal of Personality and Social Psychology,* 1967, *6,* 371–380.

Wason, P. C., and Johnson-Laird, P. N. *Psychology of Reasoning: Structure and Content.* London: Batsford, 1965.

Wicklund, R. A., and Brehm, J. W. *Perspectives on Cognitive Dissonance.* Hillsdale, N.J.: Erlbaum, 1976.

Lee Ross and Mark R. Lepper are associate professors of psychology at Stanford University.

Likeness in meaning does not predict covariation between behaviors; thus, it is hazardous to substitute propositions about language for propositions about the world.

The Systematic Distortion Hypothesis

Richard A. Shweder
Roy G. D'Andrade

Personality researchers who rely on memory-based assessment procedures (inventories, checklists, questionnaires) to study the organization of individual differences tend to discover generalized personality traits, coherent syndromes, and simple main effects (Block, 1965; Cattell, 1946; LaForge and Suczek, 1955; Norman, 1963; Smith, 1967). The systematic distortion hypothesis (D'Andrade, 1965, 1973, 1974; Shweder, 1975, 1977a, b; Shweder and D'Andrade, 1979b) suggests that much of this memory-based evidence in support of global personality trait structure is artifactual. In this chapter we examine the systematic distortion hypothesis and discuss its implications for our understanding of personality structure, human judgment, and implicit personality theory.

The Systematic Distortion Hypothesis

The systematic distortion hypothesis states that under difficult memory conditions judges on personality inventories, rating forms, and questionnaire

Research on the Brief Psychiatric Rating Scale and videotape of family interaction was carried out with support from the National Institute of Mental Health under Grant No. MN19864 to D'Andrade. An earlier version of this chapter was entitled "Personality or Culture?" Preparation of this chapter was made possible in part by a grant from the Public Health Service, PHS 5S07RR07029-13, to Shweder.

interviews infer what "must" have happened from their general beliefs about what the world is like and/or find it easier to retrieve conceptually related memory items. The hypothesis further states that our general beliefs about what the world is like in the area of personality (our implicit personality theories) tend to be inaccurate with respect to how behaviors covary, confusing "what is like what" with "what goes with what"; therefore interbehavior correlations derived from memory-based assessment procedures cannot be considered valid evidence for the objective existence of proposed personality traits, factors, or syndromes.

Informally stated, the systematic distortion hypothesis suggests that judges on memory-based personality procedures are prone to a cognitive illusion in which "propositions about language" are confused with "propositions about the world" (D'Andrade, 1965, p. 215) and likeness in meaning mistaken for co-occurrence likelihood (Shweder, 1977b; also see Chapman, 1967; Chapman and Chapman, 1967, 1969).

One way to test the systematic distortion hypothesis is to compare the degrees of correspondence between interbehavior patterns of association (for example, measures of correlation, distance, and mutual substitutability) derived from similarity of meaning judgments, memory-based hypothesis predicts that correlations *between behaviors* in memory-based personality ratings are not accurate reports about the interbehavior correlations found in actual behavior but instead reflect the degree to which the labels for the behaviors are similar in meaning.

Reproducing Memory-Based Rating Structures from Similarity of Meaning Judgments

During the last fifteen years a number of researchers have discovered that the taxonomic categories, factors, and dimensions (such as "character strength," "permissiveness," "emotional stability," "ego-resilience") induced from correlational patterns of response equivalence on standard memory-based personality instruments can also be derived by asking subjects how the items on the test are "similar in meaning" (D'Andrade, 1965, 1974, Ebbesen and Allen, 1977; Mulaik, 1964; Shweder, 1975, 1977a; see Shweder and D'Andrade, 1979b, for a review). To illustrate this procedure we have reproduced the correlational structure of a set of sixteen rating scales used in psychiatric diagnosis. The scales were developed by J. E. Overall and his associates, and are used primarily by psychiatrists and other mental health professionals for rating hospitalized patients (Overall and Hollister, 1968). Ratings are made at the end of a standard psychiatric intake interview. Reliabilities for the scales range from .56 to .86 (Overall and Gorham, 1962).

Based on cluster and factor analyses of the intercorrelations of the sixteen scales, Overall finds four "syndromes" or clusters of scales: "depressive disturbance," "thinking disturbance," "paranoid interpersonal disturbance," and "withdrawal retardation." The scales for these syndromes and factor analytic loadings, found in a number of samples, are given in Table 1.

Table 1. Brief Psychiatric Rating Scale Factor Loadings from Five Samples

		Depressive Disturbance				*Thinking Disturbance*				*Interpersonal Disturbance*				*Withdrawal Retardation*			
		VA	SN	JN	HP	VA	SN	JN	HP	VA	SN	JN	HP	VA	SN	JN	HP
Guilt	5	41	46	81	73	19	-03	00	09	02	16	-05	04	-11	09	-03	-09
Depression	9	83	50	54	80	-08	-08	-19	06	-09	08	-07	-02	-11	37	33	05
Somatic	1	70	77	56	25	04	04	-02	10	09	10	-05	04	05	-01	-03	-05
Anxiety	2	68	79	83	71	11	-02	03	24	26	26	06	22	-18	-04	-11	-11
Tension	6	34	21	42	46	13	10	17	12	24	22	15	33	04	19	08	03
Disorganized ideas	4	-25	00	07	-06	32	33	67	46	13	34	-07	22	49	35	42	21
Odd ideas	15	-19	-02	08	-04	73	58	84	82	38	64	-06	18	19	15	06	-08
Hallucinations	12	-01	02	03	-02	80	79	72	82	18	20	-24	-16	22	25	27	01
Grandiosity	8	-35	-17	-01	-29	27	08	45	27	24	44	29	32	02	-13	-13	-11
Hostility	10	03	00	15	-02	-21	-32	33	-03	85	84	79	88	-04	04	02	-06
Suspicious	11	-03	-02	23	04	19	-04	53	30	84	87	33	79	08	00	-04	-13
Uncooperative	14	-02	-16	-03	09	-17	-09	20	-13	36	28	67	45	49	53	50	57
Withdrawn	3	04	-10	-03	02	-06	-01	06	02	-02	-01	08	00	88	85	87	90
Unresponsive	16	-07	-05	-02	00	-06	-01	-02	05	-21	00	-05	-05	76	87	88	82
Slow	13	42	19	04	05	-07	-06	-22	-07	-22	-14	-16	-29	41	74	74	65
Odd gesture	7	03	01	06	-01	15	08	17	02	20	11	00	01	62	54	31	53

Source: Overall, Hollister, and Pichot, 1967.

VA = Veterans Hospital Drug Screening Data N = 725
SN = Senior Nurse Ratings N = 549
JN = Junior Nurse Ratings N = 549
HP = Hospital Psychiatrists Ratings N = 549

In order to reproduce these syndromes or clusters of scales with similarity ratings made by laymen, the semi-technical psychiatric phrasing of the original scales was translated into ordinary language. The translated scales are presented in Figure 1. Ten university undergraduates were asked to rate all pairs of scales with regard to their similarity in meaning on a + 100 to – 100 scale, where + 100 was defined as "completely identical in meaning" and – 100 was defined as "completely opposite in meaning," and zero was defined as "unrelated in meaning."

The matrices for the intercorrelations of the psychiatrists' patient ratings and the undergraduates' similarity judgments are correlated .66. U-Statistic cluster analyses (D'Andrade, 1978) of the rating scales and the similarity judgments yield very similar results (see Tables 2 and 3). Both show the four "syndromes" of anxious depression, thinking disorder, paranoid interpersonal disturbance and withdrawal retardation. Two scales change clusters in the analysis of similarity ratings. The scale labelled "uncooperative" moves from the withdrawal retardation cluster in the psychiatrists' patient ratings to the paranoid interpersonal disturbance cluster in the undergraduate similarity ratings, while the scale labelled "odd gestures" moves from the withdrawal retardation cluster to the thinking disturbance cluster. Similarity of meaning judgments yield patterns of association that are similar to the patterns found in the intercorrelations of ratings.

Accurate Reflection or Systematic Distortion?

The correspondence between similarity of meaning structures and memory-based personality rating structures is compatible with two quite

Figure 1. Short Phrases from Ordinary Language Translation of the Brief Psychiatric Rating Scale

1. concern about bodily health; health as a major problem
2. worry and anxiety about things which have happened or might happen
3. withdrawn and not emotionally involved
4. confused and disorganized ideas and ways of talking
5. guilty or remorseful feelings; concern about things that might have been done wrong
6. physically tense and jittery
7. odd gestures, facial expressions, ways of moving
8. exaggerated idea of self-importance and belief in own unusual ability
9. sad, depressed, despondent
10. full of hostile, disdainful, and belligerent feelings toward other people
11. thinks other people are (or might have been) against him or out to hurt him
12. has visions; sees or hears things that other people do not see or hear
13. slowed down in thinking, talking, or moving
14. uncooperative, unfriendly, and resentful
15. odd or strange ways of thinking
16. unresponsive and almost without emotional reactions

Table 2. Rated Behavior Structure. Correlations in Psychiatrists' Assessments of 549 Patients Using Overall's Brief Psychiatric Rating Scale

	0	1	2	6	5	9	12	8	4	15	11	10	14	7	3	16	13
Somatic concerns	1	100	21	9	22	15	1	1	3	14	7	4	-11	2	-7	3	-9
Anxiety	2	21	100	49	32	41	15	-8	5	18	30	15	-8	-3	-6	-9	-15
Physically tense	6	9	49	100	26	25	3	5	14	13	22	24	17	15	10	-6	-16
Guilt feelings	5	22	32	26	100	40	2	-4	7	10	5	5	-11	-3	-8	-3	-9
Depressed	9	15	41	25	40	100	5	-22	-5	1	4	-2	-6	-4	5	3	16
Hallucinations	12	1	15	3	2	5	100	8	17	35	13	-15	-14	2	2	3	5
Grandiosity	8	1	-8	5	-4	-22	8	100	27	39	19	28	6	1	-8	-9	-27
Disorganized ideas	4	3	5	14	7	-5	17	27	100	50	23	17	12	20	23	13	1
Unusual thoughts	15	14	18	13	10	1	35	39	50	100	33	14	6	-3	-6	-1	-22
Suspicious	11	7	30	22	5	4	13	19	23	33	100	50	14	-13	-10	-11	-25
Hostile	10	4	15	24	5	-2	-15	28	17	14	50	100	31	1	-7	-7	-29
Uncooperative	14	-11	-8	17	-11	6	-14	6	12	6	14	31	100	34	48	26	27
Odd gestures	7	2	-3	15	-3	-4	2	1	20	-3	-13	1	34	100	40	33	29
Withdrawn	3	-7	-6	10	8	5	2	-8	23	-6	-10	-7	48	40	100	62	51
Unresponsive	16	3	-9	-6	-3	3	3	-9	13	-1	-11	-7	26	33	62	100	35
Physically slow	13	-9	-15	-16	-9	16	5	-27	1	-22	-25	-29	27	29	51	36	100

Table 3. Conceptual Similarity Structure. Mean Similarity Ratings by 10 Informants (100 'always go together', 0 'unrelated', – 100 'never go together') for Modified Version of Overall's Brief Psychiatric Rating Scale

		1	2	6	5	9	12	8	4	15	7	11	10	14	3	16	13
Somatic concerns	1	100	60	20	– 5	30	– 35	– 5	– 50	– 10	– 30	20	– 10	– 65	– 25	– 55	– 90
Anxiety	2	60	100	80	70	40	10	– 55	– 10	35	60	60	10	0	– 15	– 40	– 55
Physically tense	6	20	80	100	15	– 65	10	– 10	40	15	– 25	60	15	10	– 70	– 75	– 95
Guilt feelings	5	– 5	70	15	100	80	– 15	– 50	5	0	0	5	– 35	– 30	– 20	– 75	0
Depressed	9	30	40	– 65	80	100	– 15	– 70	10	0	0	– 10	– 50	– 20	55	20	35
Hallucinations	12	– 35	10	10	– 15	– 15	100	50	40	70	30	35	5	– 25	5	– 55	– 50
Grandiosity	8	– 5	– 55	– 10	– 50	– 70	50	100	– 10	60	5	40	55	10	– 60	– 65	– 90
Disorganized ideas	4	– 50	– 10	40	5	10	40	– 10	100	80	65	25	10	– 5	20	10	5
Unusual thoughts	15	– 10	35	15	0	0	70	60	80	100	75	45	20	25	0	– 15	10
Odd gestures	7	– 30	60	– 25	0	0	30	5	65	75	100	10	0	– 35	0	– 5	0
Suspicious	11	20	60	60	5	– 10	35	40	25	45	10	100	70	60	– 5	– 65	– 60
Hostile	10	– 11	10	15	– 35	– 50	5	55	10	20	0	70	100	70	– 45	– 70	– 45
Uncooperative	14	– 65	0	10	– 30	– 20	– 25	10	– 5	25	– 35	60	70	100	40	0	– 15
Withdrawn	3	– 25	– 15	– 70	– 20	55	5	– 60	20	0	0	– 5	– 45	40	100	100	35
Unresponsive	16	– 55	– 40	– 75	– 75	20	– 55	– 65	10	– 15	– 5	– 65	– 70	0	100	100	70
Physically slow	13	– 90	– 55	– 95	0	35	– 50	– 90	5	10	0	– 60	– 45	– 15	35	70	100

divergent hypotheses. On the one hand, it is conceivable that semantic structures (patterns of conceptual association) and memory-based rating structures correspond because both are accurate reflections or encodings of what actually correlates with what in the real world. On the other hand, it is conceivable that memory-based personality ratings are systematically distorted in the direction of preexisting ideas about "what is like what" and that neither the semantic structures nor the rating structures tell us much about which behaviors correlate with each other in actual conduct.

One way to choose between the "accurate reflection" and "systematic distortion" hypotheses is to assess the degree of correspondence between the interbehavior patterns of association (clusters, traits, syndromes, or factors) derived from personality ratings and/or similarity of meaning judgments with the interbehavior patterns of association derived from a reasonably objective performance standard, such as reliable, on-line scorings of conduct. In general, comparisons of this type have supported the "systematic distortion" hypothesis (D'Andrade, 1973, 1974; Newcomb, 1929, 1931; Shweder, 1975, 1977a, b). What correlates with what in memory-based personality ratings corresponds to "what is like what" in similarity of meaning judgments and neither the rating structure nor the semantic structure tells us much about what actually correlates with what in the real world. As an illustration consider the following analysis of a thirty minute videotape of natural unstaged interaction among four members of a family.

Systematic Distortion: An Illustration

The material to be analyzed was taken from a nationally broadcast documentary series presented over public television. For over a year the ordinary and extraordinary events in the life of a white upper middle class California family were videotaped. From this record, twelve hour-length shows were produced. For this study, thirty minutes were selected from the last hour in which Pat and Bill, the mother and father of the family, and Lance and Delilah, the oldest son and the oldest daughter, appeared.

For the purpose of comparing what correlated with what in actual behavior and in memory-based ratings, it was important to select a set of relatively unambiguous everyday terms for describing interpersonal behavior. It was also important to select terms whose application occurred frequently enough to establish differences between the four people or "actors" to be scored and rated. A preliminary list of forty-five terms was taken from Osgood's semantic analysis of interpersonal behavior terms (Osgood, 1970). Using the transcripts and the videotape, two scorers were asked to determine each time an actor completed an act, and then to check on Osgood's list the term or terms they thought described the behavior. Using this procedure, the sixteen highest frequency terms were selected.

The next step was to have a set of on-line, immediate scorings made by three coders using just the sixteen terms. Again the scorers were asked to determine the boundaries of each act using the transcript and viewing the tape, and then check on the list of sixteen terms the term or terms which characterized each act. On the average, the three scorers coded three hundred and sixty-nine acts following this procedure. Informal inspection of the coded transcripts indicates that the raters agreed in most cases on the segmentation of particular acts, apparently because the turn-taking system of natural conversation functions as an act-segmenting device.

Reliabilities were derived from the average of the product-moment correlations between pairs of scorers for each category of interpersonal behavior using percentages of acts across actors. The correlations were averaged for the three pairs of scorers using Fisher's r to Z transformation. The mean correlations are presented in Table 4.

Examination of the reliability figure scores across the four actors indicated that two of the categories were unreliable: "explain," with a mean r of $-.42$ and "support," with a mean r of $-.40$. For three other categories, the percents of acts were identical for all actors: "lead," "warn," and "be courteous." These five categories were dropped from the analysis.

For the memory-based rating condition, twenty university undergraduates viewed the tape. No more than three subjects viewed the tape at the same time. When two or more subjects viewed the tape together they were instructed not to talk about it and to refrain from showing any reaction. As each of the four actors appeared on the screen they were identified by the experimenter. Subjects were told that they would be given a questionnaire about the behavior and actions of the actors after the tape was finished. The questionnaire was administered immediately upon completion of the tape. On each page of the questionnaire the actor's name was written along with scales

Table 4. Product Moment Correlations Between Pairs of Scorers Across Actors by Behavior Category

Category	*Scorer 1 and 2*	*Scorer 1 and 3*	*Scorer 2 and 3*	*Mean r*
1. inform	.54	.23	.73	.53
2. question	.99	.98	.99	.99
3. explain	.12	.24	−.93	−.40
4. joke	.84	.73	.97	.89
5. criticize	.97	.86	.81	.91
6. agree	.83	.24	.04	.45
7. disagree	.70	.99	.79	.91
8. advise	.74	.53	.95	.82
9. ridicule	.99	.97	.98	.98
10. suggest	−.22	.79	.21	.34
11. praise	.53	.74	.94	.80
12. lead	.69	.79	.99	.91
13. warn	.81	.96	.93	.92
14. support	.26	−.23	−.03	−.00
15. comply	.61	.71	.77	.70
16. be courteous	.46	.59	.90	.71

for each behavior category. Raters were asked "How much does [so-and-so] do the following [for example, inform others]?" Ratings were made on a seven point scale (1 = not at all; 7 = a lot).

For each judge in the memory-based rating condition, Kendall's tau was computed for all pairs of categories across actors. To compute tau for a pair of categories, each judge's ratings were used to obtain a rank ordering of the four actors on both categories, and tau was then computed from the two rank orderings. Tau coefficients were then averaged across the twenty judges for each pair of categories. The matrix of mean tau coefficients is presented in Table 5.

To obtain a correlation matrix for the immediate on-line scorings, mean percentage figures were used to rank order actors on each category. Tau coefficients were computed from the rank orders for all pairs of categories. The results are also presented in Table 5.

By inspection it can be seen that the pattern of association for the memory-based ratings is quite different than the pattern of association for the immediate scorings. The lines in Table 5 represent the major clusters discovered in a U-Statistic cluster analysis of similarity of meaning judgments for these categories. The product moment correlation between the matrix for memory-based ratings and the matrix for immediate scorings of behavior (Table 5) is only .22.

In order to compare the interbehavior correlations derived from both immediate, on-line scoring, and memory-based ratings with judgments of semantic similarity, judgments were obtained from ten undergraduates for all pairs of eleven categories on a scale running from "identical in meaning" to "completely opposite in meaning." The intervals of the scale ran from + 100 to – 100. The mean judgments are presented in Table 6.

The matrix for the similarity of meaning judgments is similar in its pattern of associations to the matrix for the memory-based ratings (r = .75), but

Figure 2. Degrees of Correspondence (Pearson r) Between Correlational Structures Derived from Similarity of Meaning Judgments (Semantic Structure), Memory-Based Ratings (Rating Structure), and Immediate Scorings (Behavioral Structure) in Videotape Study

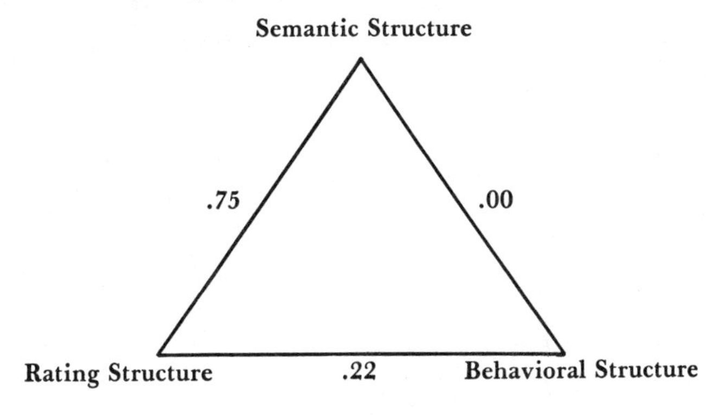

Table 5. Mean Tau Coefficients for Actor Rank Orders Derived from Memory-Based Ratings (Upper Half Matrix) and Tau Coefficients for Actor Rank Orders Derived from Immediate Scorings (Lower Half Matrix)

	ag	*co*	*pr*	*ad*	*in*	*su*	*qu*	*cr*	*di*	*jo*	*ri*
Agree	*	.28	.29	.07	.11	.06	−.01	−.31	−.42	.16	−.24
Comply	−.67	*	.39	.07	.11	.12	−.11	−.31	−.18	−.25	−.50
Praise	.00	.33	*	.08	−.05	.03	−.06	−.46	−.31	.21	−.27
Advise	.33	−.67	−.67	*	.42	.51	.24	.10	.05	−.33	−.03
Inform	.00	−.33	.33	.00	*	.37	.14	.00	−.10	−.21	−.24
Suggest	−.67	.33	−.33	.00	−.33	*	.11	.13	−.02	−.49	−.29
Question	−.67	.33	.33	.00	.33	.33	*	.12	−.01	−.19	−.13
Criticize	.00	−.33	−1.00	.67	−.33	.33	−.33	*	.59	−.30	.39
Disagree	1.00	−.67	.00	.33	.00	−.67	−.67	.00	*	−.11	.45
Joke	.00	.33	.33	−.67	−.33	−.33	−.33	−.33	.00	*	.17
Ridicule	.33	.00	−.67	.33	−.67	.00	−.67	.67	.33	.00	*

Table 6. Mean Conceptual Similarity Ratings, 10 Subjects

	ag	*co*	*pr*	*ad*	*in*	*su*	*qu*	*cr*	*di*	*jo*	*ri*
Agree	*	68	60	- 16	- 16	04	- 36	- 60	- 32	- 44	- 56
Comply	68	*	36	04	- 12	- 32	- 36	- 60	- 56	- 56	- 44
Priase	60	36	*	- 28	- 36	12	- 32	- 40	- 52	00	- 44
Advise	- 16	04	- 28	*	76	88	- 04	- 08	- 36	- 44	- 36
Inform	- 16	- 12	- 36	76	*	64	- 12	- 12	- 28	- 52	- 36
Suggest	04	- 32	12	88	64	*	- 16	- 28	16	- 36	- 44
Question	- 36	- 36	- 32	- 04	- 12	- 16	*	44	72	- 40	- 20
Criticize	- 60	- 60	- 40	- 08	- 12	- 28	44	*	44	- 04	80
Disagree	- 32	- 56	- 52	- 36	- 28	16	72	44	*	- 16	24
Joke	- 44	- 56	00	-44	- 52	- 36	- 40	- 04	- 16	*	88
Ridicule	- 56	- 44	- 44	- 36	- 36	- 44	- 20	80	24	88	*

not at all like the matrix for the immediate scorings of behavior (r = .00). (And, as already noted, the latter two matrices correlate only .22.) What we discover in these various comparisons of memory-based rating structure, actual behavior structure, and conceptual similarity structure is predicted by the "systematic distortion" hypothesis. That is, there appears to be a systematic bias in memory. Correlations between categories in memory-based ratings reflect the degree to which the categories are similar in meaning, rather than the relationships found in immediately scored behavior. See Figure 2.

Implications for Studies of Personality Structure

In the personality literature, much of the evidence for the existence of global personality traits, syndromes, or factors is based on interbehavior correlational evidence derived from memory-based ratings. The systematic distortion hypothesis suggests that such evidence cannot be trusted. The hypothesis challenges us to construct a portrait of personality structure based instead on on-line records of conduct.

It seems likely that a shift in research methods from memory-based assessment procedures to behavioral observational techniques will alter our understanding of personality structure. Most researchers who utilize immediate, on-line scorings techniques to study the organization of individual differences tend to discover complex person-context-response mode interaction effects and undramatic interbehavior correlations.

Broad, empirically homogeneous multi-item traits or syndromes (for example, extrovert: likes parties, feels at ease talking before a group, introduces himself to strangers) are difficult to induce from behavior observational evidence (Mischel, 1968; Moos, 1969; Newcomb, 1929; Raush, Dittmann, and Taylor, 1959; Sears, 1963; Yarrow and Waxler, 1976). Instead, one discovers that *minor changes in context, task, or response mode produce major changes in individual difference rankings* (Campbell and Fiske, 1959; Cronbach, 1975; Fiske, 1978; Mischel, 1968; Moos, 1969; Newcomb, 1929; Raush, Dittmann, and Taylor, 1959; Shweder, 1979a; Slovic, 1972b).

The Whitings' findings (1975, p. 163, for example,) are representative of available behavior observational evidence on the generalization of individual differences across *contexts.* In a study of children's social behavior to peers, infants, and adults, the highest level of cross-contextual generalization for a purported trait of behavior was .29 (Pearson r; n = 134). For the response tendency "nurturance" the degree of generalization was .05. Knowing that a child is relatively more nurturant than others *to adults,* for example, tells you little about whether he will be relatively more nuturant than others *to peers.*

Sears' findings (1963) are representative of available behavior observational evidence on the generalization of individual differences across *response modes.* In a study of "dependency" in children, Sears discovered that, on the average, "similar" response modes (such as seeks attention, seeks help, seeks physical nearness) intercorrelated .21. Children who seek attention more than others from their mothers are not much more likely than other children to "cling to their mothers' apron strings."

How sensitive are individual difference rankings to variations in context (time, place, personnel), task, and response mode? At the moment this is unclear (although for a despairing view see Cronbach, 1975). What does seem clear is that the world of individual differences in behavior is not organized in the way envisioned by personality trait theorists. Individual differences exist, of course, but they do not seem to generalize widely across similar contexts, tasks, or response modes. As Slovic (1972b) remarks in his review of the evidence against the existence of the purported trait, "risk-taker," as a generalized response tendency of individuals: "Only those tasks highly similar in structure and involving the same sorts of payoffs (all financial, all social) have shown any generality . . . and, as similarity decreases, these intertask correlations rapidly decrease . . ." (p. 128).

In summary, when one has a reasonably objective performance standard (such as on-line scorings of a videotape) on individual differences across comparable contexts, tasks, and response modes, what one discovers is a world of complex statistical interaction effects, multiple necessary conditions, and insubstantial intercorrelations among events. We may well live in a world where a relevant disposition is the tendency for middle-aged men to get angry when extravagantly dressed middle-aged women cut in front of them in line, but this regularity in someone's conduct may tell us little about whether he is more likely than others to get angry when contradicted in an argument at a scientific meeting.

Notably, this complex organization of individual differences is *not* encoded in implicit personality theory, and is rarely reported on personality rating forms, inventories, or questionnaires. Quite the contrary, our everyday theories of what goes with what in personality ("friendly" and "smiles a lot" go together; "gentle" and "managerial" exclude one another) portray a world of neat clusters, simple main effects, and widely generalized regularities. It is that conceptually coherent, neatly integrated portrait of the organization of individual differences that judges seem to report on memory-based personality tests (see D'Andrade, 1965; LaForge and Suczek, 1955; Mulaik, 1964; Norman, 1963; Passini and Norman, 1966; Shweder, 1975).

Implications for the Study of Human Judgment

The systematic distortion hypothesis states that judges on personality instruments have difficulty remembering the correlational structure of observed behavioral events. One implication of the hypothesis, supported by some recent research on "probability learning," is that human learning mechanisms do not guarantee insight into the "statistical structure of sequences of events" (Estes, 1976a, p. 51). (See also Einhorn and Hogarth, 1978.) Individual observers are not skillful at arriving at a vertical understanding of the contingencies in their environment.

This is not only true for event sequences with complex statistical structures; it seems that observers readily comprehend the contingent structure of experience only under quite special circumstances (Estes, 1976a, b). As one study of correlational thinking concludes, "those who receive information on a trial by trial basis, as it usually occurs in the real world, generally fail to assess adequately the degree of relationship present" (Ward and Jenkins, 1965, p. 240; also see Einhorn and Hogarth, 1978; Jenkins and Ward, 1965; Shweder, 1977c; Slovic, 1972a; Smedslund, 1963).

Recent research on probability learning contains three related messages: (1) Judges often assess "the probability of an event by the ease with which instances or occurrences can be brought to mind" (Tversky and Kahneman, 1974, p. 1127; see also 1973); (2) Event categories are sometimes encoded, accessed, and retrieved, that is, "brought to mind," according to principles unrelated to event probabilities, thereby resulting in erroneous estimations of event likelihoods; (3) Two of the potentially hazardous principles for encoding, accessing, and retrieving event categories are "relative frequency" (Estes, 1976a, b) and "verbal association strength" or "conceptual affiliation" (Chapman, 1967; Chapman and Chapman, 1967, 1969).

Tversky and Kahneman (1974), for example, in a discussion of human predictive behavior, describe a number of techniques relied on by judges to estimate event likelihoods. One very general technique is known as the "availability heuristic": people assess "the probability of an event by the ease with which instances or occurrences can be brought to mind," as noted earlier.

Tversky and Kahneman argue that the availability heuristic is relied on in estimation tasks because "lifelong experience has taught us that, in general, instances of large classes are recalled better and faster than instances of less frequent classes; that likely occurrences are easier to imagine than unlikely ones . . ." (1974, p. 1128). Tversky and Kahneman are quick to point out, however, that there are many influences on the ease with which instances of an event class can be brought to mind, and since many of these influences are unrelated to the probability of an event, the availability heuristic has the potential to produce massive and systematic biases in judgment.

Just how hazardous it is to rely on the availability heuristic is made apparent by Estes (1976a) who suggests that more likely occurrences are not easier to bring to mind than less likely occurrences unless the more likely occurrence also happens to be the more frequent occurrence. As Estes notes: human predictive behavior is (p. 45) "not a probability estimate but rather a record in memory of past frequencies of events": *subjects invariably rely on relative frequency information to estimate the probabilities of events even when relative frequency information is unrelated to event likelihoods.* Certain classes of events that are relevant for probability estimation, that is, the number of times an event that might have occurred did *not* occur, are just not processed. It is not more *likely* events that are easier to retrieve but more *frequent* ones. The availability heuristic would seem to be a "rational" technique for estimating event likelihoods only if the relative frequency of an event happens to correlate with its likelihood.

It can be dangerous to rely on an accurate relative frequency sensor when estimating the likelihood of an event. For example, in one experiment Estes (1976a) permitted subjects to observe a contest in which A was pitted against B 100 times with a .75 probability of success (A won 75 times) while C was pitted against D 200 times with a .50 probability of success (C won 100 times). Subjects were then asked to predict the results of an uncertain event: who will win if A is pitted against C? As Estes (1976a) notes: "it seems clear that if he bases his prediction on rational grounds he should predict A over C, and at worst, if he is unable to transfer acquired information to the test situation, he should mentally toss a coin and predict A or C with equal probabilities" (p. 43).

Neither "rational" prediction occurred. Despite the fact that A had won a greater proportion of contests against its opponents (75 out of 100) than C had won against its opponents (100 out of 200) in every instance subjects predicted the winner of the A versus C contest to be C, "the stimulus that accumulated the largest number of wins during the observation series regardless of its (past) probability of winning or losing" (Estes, 1976a, p. 44). Subjects failed to process information about two rather large classes of events, the number of *losses* incurred by A and C, that is, the number of times victory did *not* occur.

Reliance on relative frequency information makes sense if relevant events have had an equal number of opportunities to occur or not occur. As Estes (1976a) notes, if the relative frequency of an event happens to correspond to its probability of occurrence (which would have been the case had Estes' subjects witnessed an *equal* number of observation trials for A versus B, and C versus D) then reliance on relative frequency information will lead judges "to make judgments that appear to reflect differences in probabilities of events with great fidelity, but, under slightly different circumstances [for example, when cue frequencies are unequal and frequency of occurrence is unrelated to likelihood of occurrence], the equally efficient operation of the same learning process leads (subjects) to make judgments of likelihoods of events that are widely at variance with the actual probabilities" (p. 51). It is not known how far one can get in our world by deriving predictions of event likelihoods simply from information about relative frequency, but it is clear that the strategy is fraught with dangers.

Estes' research demonstrates that human judges have difficulty with simple comparative proportional estimations. It is therefore not surprising that judges are disinclined to compare conditional probabilities or to process correlation relevant information (see Jenkins and Ward, 1965; Slovic, 1972a; Shweder, 1977c; Ward and Jenkins, 1965). Other, more complex, manipulations of frequency information (such as arriving at an estimate of the proportional *reduction* of error in predicting values on one variable given knowledge of values on a second variable—see Hayes, 1963, p. 608, on the logic of predictive association) are probably beyond the intuitive information processing inclinations of most intelligent adults.

A second hazardous principle for encoding event categories in probability estimation tasks is "verbal association strength" or "conceptual affiliation." Consider the following example:

Which inference would you endorse?
M. G. has self-esteem. Therefore, M. G. probably is *not* a leader.
M. G. has self esteem. Therefore, M. G. probably *is* a leader.

Most informants endorse the second inference. Why? Have they accessed their own frequency beliefs about the conditional probability of being versus not being a leader given that you have self-esteem? If they had, they would have discovered that according to their own beliefs "most people with self-esteem are not leaders" (Shweder, 1977c). Therefore M. G. probably is *not* a leader. What went wrong?

When informants tell us that self-esteem and leadership go together, or draw the inference that someone with self-esteem is likely to be a leader, they are not processing information about the correlation of two variables or the conditional probability of one given the other. What they are doing is judging the extent to which two events co-occur by the extent to which the events affiliate in their minds or have strong verbal associative connections. The conceptual linkages among event classes are relied on to estimate their contingent relationship across persons. Often the result is an "illusory correlation," a consensual estimate of the inductive relationship among events that is not warranted by experience (see Chapman, 1967; Chapman and Chapman, 1967, 1969; D'Andrade, 1974; Shweder, 1975, 1977a; Tversky and Kahneman, 1974). Self-esteem and leadership, for example, go together in our culture's portrait of the ideal leader and in various personifications of that ideal (for example, F. D. R., John Kennedy): They hardly correlate at all across personalities.

There are many ways objects and events conceptually affiliate in our minds. Flavell and Stedman (1961) identify eleven types of "logico-grammatical" relationships for defining the connection between words. These include "similarity" (damp–wet), "supraordination" (animal–fox), "action of" (lion–roar), "action upon" (throw–ball), and "whole-part" (shoe–heel). Casagrande and Hale (1967) needed thirteen types of "semantic relationships" to adequately describe the folk definitions of their Papago Indian informants. These include definition by reference to action sequences, function, common attribute, and so on. If one is asked how two things "go together" there are obviously many legitimate ways to reply.

In general, conceptual affiliation is a poor index of co-occurence likelihood. Things can be alike without co-occurring. Things can co-occur without being alike. Things can go together in an action sequence without correlating over personalities. For example, blue and green are both alike in hue but that does not entitle us to infer that they co-vary as attributes of "colored things." Similarly, "clings to his mother's apron strings" and "seeks help" are both kinds of "dependent" things to do; they conceptually affiliate in our minds as subordinates of the same category "dependent." Yet this type of conceptual connectedness tells us little about whether those children who "cling to their mother's apron strings" are also the ones who "seek help." The various and diverse ways objects and events relate in our minds is not isomorphic with information about conditional or joint conditional probabilities. A likeness is not a likelihood.

The evidence that we are not intuitively skillful at probability estimation may, at first blush, seem implausible. Many of us seem to assume unwittingly that, over the course of evolutionary history, human survival has, in some way, depended upon our ability to perform high order feats of inductive inferring and probabilistic estimation. Since our species has obviously survived, at least until now, adherence to this assumption makes it necessary to resist or doubt evidence of our limited ability to engage in inductive (and deductive) reasoning or draw correlational lessons from experience.

We would recommend an alternative assumption. In the light of increasing evidence that most intelligent adults are not intuitively inclined to formal operational thinking (see Wason and Johnson-Laird, 1972), we find it preferable to assume that adaptive processes do not require a high level of formal propositional thinking.

Much of the knowledge we possess (and we do possess valid knowledge) is organized in very mundane ways and requires relatively low level inference. Some of this knowledge is episodic and script-like (see Schank and Abelson, 1977); we know what will follow what in a chain of time. Some of it is repetitive and context-specific; we know how so-and-so behaved last time under such-and-such circumstances. There is no necessary reason to assume that mankind's potential for rational adaptive behavior can only be derived in one way, for instance, from some supposed formal operation-like inductive (and deductive) capacity of the individual human mind. In the past, perhaps even today, the context-specific intellectual demands of everyday life may not be very great.

On the other hand, it would be a mistake to conclude that we are always inaccurate in our probability estimations or that we never gain insight into the contingent relationships among events. Estes' point, as we read it, is that it is possible for a God, nature, the environment, or an experimenter, wittingly or unwittingly, to arrange events (for example, by equalizing cue frequencies) so that exclusive reliance on relative frequency information is an accurate index of event likelihoods. There may even be occasions when verbal association strength and contingency happen to be isomorphic. That is, God, nature, the environment, or an experimenter can help us appear more impressive than we are at probability estimation; even accuracy can be an artifact.

Moreover, Azjen (1977), Tversky and Kahneman (1978), and Ward and Jenkins (1965) have shown that task characteristics can be arranged so that probabilistic and correlational evidence can be easily fit into a pre-existing causal schema or script. Well-scripted evidence is easier to process.

In summary there are two related points to be made about human judgment. The first is that the very same rather limited learning mechanisms and information processing skills can interact with the demands of particular tasks to yield either accurate assessments of reality or massively biased estimations. The second point is that human observers are not infrequently out of accord with the causal and contingent structure of their environment.

Implications for the Study of Implicit Personality Theory

There is a widespread assumption in personality psychology that the lexical items of implicit personality theory (such as honest, responsible, industrious, cooperative, friendly) are labels for scientific categories. Everyday trait terms are often appropriated into academic discourse as though they were inductive summary formulas about the organization of individual differences which encode information about empirical affinities (self-reliant/responsible) and exclusions (gregarious/reserved), and thus have utility in predicting future events and minimizing surprise (Brown, 1965, p. 612; Jackson, Chan, and Stricker, 1979; Passini and Norman, 1966). The systematic distortion hypothesis raises the possibility that the personality categories and classifications of everyday life may not be designed to serve the needs of "man-as-scientist," and should not be analyzed, evaluated, or used as though they were scientific schemes.

Scientists construct classifications and categories for the sake of drawing inductive generalizations ("things that are hot" are "things that hurt;" "people who like parties" are "people who introduce themselves to strangers"—Gilmour, 1937, p. 1040; see also Gilmour, 1951). Given this goal, it follows that the primary criterion for judging the adequacy of a scientific classification is that it be "founded on attributes which have a number of other attributes correlated with them . . ." (Gilmour, 1937, p. 1040). It is important to recognize, especially when studying mundane social cognition, that not all classifications or categories are inductive in intent or designed to serve the inferential purposes of "man-as-scientist."

Many of the conceptual schemes of everyday life are prescriptive (normative) not descriptive in their intent (see Mischel, 1964). They provide "models for" not "models of" reality (Geertz, 1973). They organize the world into categories of events, things, and people for the sake of telling the world how it ought to behave. Since much of human conduct is regulated by rules it would not be surprising if most of the conceptual schemes of everyday life, including implicit personality "theories" (a misnomer?), served a normative purpose, at least in part. What is a "dog?" Among other things, that's a potentially nutritious animal that one should not eat. *Modern Etiquette in Private and Public* (1872) tells us something about the category "fish." At a dinner party it is to be served directly after the soup, and "you must eat it with a fork, unless silver knives are provided." Science is not all there is to cognition. Mapping correlational structure is not all that the categories of everyday life are about.

There are many non-scientific functions served by our lexicon for personality trait categories. Trait terms are used to inspire conduct ("be courageous"), to proscribe conduct ("stop being so dependent"), and to influence the way others will react. Personality trait labels and trait talk may serve rhetorical, persuasive, and regulatory functions more admirably than they serve predictive or inductive functions.

One can also speculate that personality trait talk serves an important symbolic function in a voluntaristic, individualistic culture like our own. The way a culture allocates individuals to positions in social groups (who is accepted, promoted, retained, confided in, allied with, delegated power and responsibility) expresses or says something about its values, goals, and its views of what is important in man and society. Entrenched Western values make it reprehensible to accept, hire, or promote, either blindly or on the basis of family connections, birthright, color, or caste. Neither a random number table nor a genealogical tree is the right kind of symbol for the image of autonomous man enshrined in Western culture. Selection on the basis of personal character, not chance or connections, is part of our culture's mythic self-conception.

Thus, a priori, there seems to be no reason to assume that everyday personality categories have evolved to serve scientific goals, or to assume that the cultural practices in which trait labels play a part are primarily scientific practices. Everyday trait and type categories (trustworthy, responsible, "the spoiled child") may exist for reasons other than summarizing or encoding nature's regularities. This point is especially important because it implies that the stability and persistence of implicit personality "theories" may be unrelated to the issue of empirical homogeneity and nomological network. One should not expect our everyday trait lexicon to go away simply because it fails to yield valid predictions about what correlates with what across personalities, nor should one doubt that our trait lexicon fails to yield valid predictions simply because it has not gone away.

Summary and a Caution

The systematic distortion hypothesis states that the pattern of correlations among items on memory-based personality instruments tells us more about diverse forms of conceptual affiliation in the minds of raters than about what actually correlates with what across individual differences in conduct, and that these forms of conceptual affiliation can be most easily discovered by simply asking a handful of informants "what is like what?" Examination of the correlational structure of psychiatric ratings using categories from the "Brief Psychiatric Rating Scale" revealed that this rating structure could be reproduced from semantic judgments about "similarity in meaning." Examination of thirty minutes of videotaped interaction among members of a family revealed that memory-based rating structures parallel pre-existing similarity of meaning structures but do not accurately reflect the correlational structure of actual behavior. Three implications of the systematic distortion hypothesis were discussed:

1. Individual differences are narrowly context-dependent. The neat trait categories and factors so easily retrieved by asking "what is like what" or by examining memory-based rating data are often difficult to induce from actual performance criteria.

2. Normal, intelligent adults are not intuitively skillful at estimating the probability of an event (unless the relative frequency of the event happens to correspond to its likelihood) or the co-occurrence probability of two events (unless the verbal associative bond connecting the two events happens to correspond to their co-occurrence probability).

3. The behavioral categories encoded in our everyday trait lexicon may not have evolved to summarize information about the organization of individual differences, and should not be interpreted as scientific categories.

We conclude this discussion of the systematic distortion hypothesis with a mild caveat: Let the reader beware.

It does not follow from the systematic distortion hypothesis that judges have not tried to faithfully report what they know, or that they know nothing about the ratee, or that any particular item judgment they make is typically erroneous. The point is *not* that raters are characteristically inaccurate. In the videotape study reported earlier, memory-based ratings of *particular* items correlated on the average .30 with measures derived from immediate scorings and in Newcomb's (1929) data rating-scoring correlations for particular items correlated in the .40 to .50 range; presumably, under special conditions favorable to our impressive relative frequency sensors, ratings could correspond even more highly to performance criteria.

The real point is that (1) raters are far from perfect (except under those special circumstances discussed earlier) and when raters do make errors their errors are *systematically biased* errors, not random errors; (2) the typical personality rating situation requires the judge to abstract and summarize a mass of observations from perhaps days, weeks, or months of observation on multiple categories that vary in their base rates and cue frequencies; numerous opportunities for error, and thus systematic bias, occur; (3) if one were to eliminate error and systematic bias from personality data one would not discover neat traits, factors, and dimensions, but rather a complex of context-dependent truths, or alternatively said, that which *is* accurate in personality ratings would not suport a global trait approach to individual differences in conduct.

References

Azjen, I. "Intuitive Theories of Events and the Effects of Base-Rate Information on Prediction." *Journal of Personality and Social Psychology,* 1977, *35,* 303–314.

Block, J. *The Challenge of Response Sets.* New York: Appleton-Century-Crofts, 1965.

Brown, R. *Social Psychology.* New York: Free Press, 1965.
Campbell, D. T., and Fiske, D. W. "Convergent and Discriminant Validation by the Multitrait-Multimethod Matrix." *Psychological Bulletin,* 1959, *56,* 81–105.
Casagrande, J. B., and Hale, K. L. "Semantic Relationships in Papago Folk-Definitions." In D. Hymes (Ed.), *Studies in Southwestern Ethnolinguistics.* The Hague: Mouton, 1967.
Cattell, R. D. *Description and Measurement of Personality.* New York: World Book, 1946.
Chapman, L. J. "Illusory Correlation in Observational Report." *Journal of Verbal Learning and Verbal Behavior,* 1967, *6,* 151–155.
Chapman, L. J., and Chapman, J. P. "Genesis of Popular but Erroneous Psychodiagnostic Observations." *Journal of Abnormal Psychology,* 1967, *72,* 193–204.
Chapman, L. J., and Chapman, J. P. "Illusory Correlation as an Obstacle to the Use of Valid Psychodiagnostic Signs." *Journal of Abnormal Psychology,* 1969, *74,* 271–280.
Cronbach, L. J. "Beyond the Two Scientific Disciplines of Scientific Psychology." *American Psychologist,* 1975, *30,* 116–127.
D'Andrade, R. G. "Trait Psychology and Componental Analysis." *American Anthropologist,* 1965, *67,* 215–228.
D'Andrade, R. G. "Cultural Constructions of Reality." In L. Nader and T. W. Maretzki (Eds.), *Cultural Illness and Health.* Washington, D.C.: American Anthropological Association, 1973.
D'Andrade, R. G. "Memory and the Assessment of Behavior." In T. Blalock (Ed.), *Measurement in the Social Sciences.* Chicago: Aldine-Atherton, 1974.
D'Andrade, R. G. "U-Statistical Hierarchical Clustering." *Psychometrica,* 1978, *43,* 59–67.
Douglas, M. *Rules and Meanings.* London: Penguin, 1973.
Ebbesen, E. B., and Allen, R. B. "Further Evidence Concerning Fiske's Question: 'Can Personality Constructs Ever Be Validated?' " Unpublished manuscript, Department of Psychology, University of California, San Diego, 1977.
Einhorn, H. J., and Hogarth, R. M. "Confidence in Judgment: Persistence of the Illusion of Validity." *Psychological Review,* 1978, *85,* 395–416.
Estes, W. K. "The Cognitive Side of Probability Learning." *Psychological Review,* 1976a, *83,* 37–64.
Estes, W. K. "Some Functions of Memory in Probability Learning and Choice Behavior." In G. H. Bower (Ed.), *The Psychology of Learning and Motivation.* Vol. 10. New York: Academic Press, 1976b.
Fiske, D. W. *Strategies for Personality Research: The Observation Versus Interpretation of Behavior.* San Francisco: Jossey-Bass, 1978.
Flavell, J. H., and Stedman, D. J. "A Developmental Study of Judgments of Semantic Similarity." *The Journal of Genetic Psychology,* 1961, *98,* 279–293.
Geertz, C. *The Interpretation of Cultures.* New York: Basic Books, 1973.
Gilmour, J. S. L. "A Taxonomic Problem." *Nature,* 1937, *139,* 1040–1042.
Gilmour, J. S. L. "The Development of Taxonomic Theory Since 1851." *Nature,* 1951, *168,* 400–402.
Hayes, W. L. *Statistics for Psychologists.* New York: Holt, Rinehart and Winston, 1963.
Jackson, D. N., Chan, D. W., and Stricker, L. J. "Implicit Personality Theory: Is It Illusory?" *Journal of Personality,* 1979, *47,* 1–10.
Jenkins, H. M., and Ward, W. C. "Judgment of Contingency Between Responses and Outcomes." *Psychological Monographs,* 1965, *79,* 1–17.
LaForge, R., and Suczek, R. F. "The Interpersonal Dimension of Personality: III, An Interpersonal Checklist." *Journal of Personality,* 1955, *24,* 94–112.
Mischel, T. "Personal Constructs, Rules, and the Logic of Clinical Activity." *Psychological Review,* 1964, *71,* 180–192.
Mischel, W. *Personality and Assessment.* New York: Wiley, 1968.

Mischel, W. "Towards a Cognitive Social Learning Reconceptualization of Personality." *Psychological Review,* 1973, *80,* 252-283.

Modern Etiquette in Private and Public. London: Warne, 1872.

Moos, R. H. "Sources of Variance in Responses to Questionnaires and in Behavior." *Journal of Abnormal Psychology,* 1969, *74,* 405-412.

Mulaik, S. A. "Are Personality Factors Raters' Conceptual Factors?" *Journal of Consulting Psychology,* 1964, *28,* 506-511.

Newcomb, T. M. "The Consistency of Certain Extrovert-Introvert Behavior Patterns in 51 Problem Boys." *Contributions to Education,* 1929, *382.*

Newcomb, T. M. "An Experiment Designed to Test the Validity of a Rating Technique." *Journal of Educational Psychology,* 1931, *32,* 279-289.

Norman, W. T. "Toward an Adequate Taxonomy of Personality Attributes: Replicated Factor Structure in Peer Nomination Personality Ratings." *Journal of Abnormal and Social Psychology,* 1963, *66,* 574-83.

Osgood, C. E. "Interpersonal Verbs and Interpersonal Behavior." In J. L. Cowan (Ed.), *Studies in Thought and Language.* Tucson: University of Arizona Press, 1970.

Overall, J. E., and Gorham, D. R. "The Brief Psychiatric Rating Scale." *Psychological Reports,* 1962, *10,* 799-812.

Overall, J. E., and Hollister, L. E. "Studies of Quantitative Approaches to Psychiatric Classification." In M. M. Katz, J. O. Cole, and W. E. Barton (Eds.), *The Role and Methodology of Classification in Psychiatry and Psychotherapy* (U.S. Public Health Service Publication No. 1584). Washington, D.C.: U.S. Government Printing Office, 1968.

Overall, J. E., Hollister, L. E., and Pichot, P. "Major Psychiatric Disorders: A Four-Dimensional Model." *Archives of General Psychiatry,* 1967, *16,* 146-151.

Passini, F. T., and Norman, W. T. "A Universal Conception of Personality Structure?" *Journal of Personality and Social Psychology,* 1966, *4,* 44-49.

Raush, H. L., Dittmann, A. T., and Taylor, T. J. "Person, Setting, and Change in Social Interaction." *Human Relations,* 1959, *12,* 361-377.

Schank, R., and Abelson, R. *Scripts, Plans, Goals, and Understanding.* Hillsdale, N.J.: Erlbaum, 1977.

Sears, R. R. "Dependency Motivation." In M. R. Jones (Ed.), *Nebraska Symposium on Motivation.* Lincoln: University of Nebraska Press, 1963.

Shweder, R. A. "Semantic Structures and Personality Assessment." Doctoral dissertation, Department of Social Relations, Harvard University. University Microfilms, Ann Arbor, Michigan. Order No. 72-29, 584, 1972.

Shweder, R. A. "How Relevant Is an Individual Difference Theory of Personality?" *Journal of Personality,* 1975, *43,* 455-484.

Shweder, R. A. "Illusory Correlation and the M. M. P. I. Controversy." *Journal of Consulting and Clinical Psychology,* 1977a, *45,* 917-924.

Shweder, R. A. "Illusory Correlation and the M. M. P. I. Controversy: Author's Reply to Some of the Allusions and Elusions in Block's and Edwards' Commentaries." *Journal of Consulting and Clinical Psychology,* 1977b, *45,* 936-940.

Shweder, R. A. "Likeness and Likelihood in Everyday Thought: Magical Thinking in Judgments about Personality." *Current Anthropology,* 1977c, *18,* 637-648.

Shweder, R. A. "Rethinking Culture and Personality Theory, Part I: A Critical Examination of Two Classical Postulates." *Ethos: Journal of the Society for Psychological Anthropology,* 1979a, *7,* 255-278.

Shweder, R. A., and D'Andrade, R. G. "Accurate Reflection or Systematic Distortion? A Reply to Block, Weiss, and Thorne." *Journal of Personality and Social Psychology,* 1979b, *37,* 1075-1084.

Slovic, P. "From Shakespeare to Simon: Speculations—and Some Evidence—About Man's Ability to Process Information." Oregon Research Institute. Research Monograph Vol. 12, No. 12, 1972a.

Slovic, P. "Information Processing, Situation Specificity, and the Generality of Risk-Taking Behavior." *Journal of Personality and Social Psychology,* 1972b, *22,* 128–134.
Smedslund, J. "The Concept of Correlation in Adults." *Scandinavian Journal of Psychology,* 1963, *4,* 165–173.
Smith, G. M. "Usefulness of Peer Ratings of Personality in Educational Research." *Educational and Psychological Measurement,* 1967, *27,* 967–984.
Tversky, A., and Kahneman, D. "Availability: A Heuristic for Judging Frequency and Probability." *Cognitive Psychology,* 1973, *5,* 207–232.
Tversky, A., and Kahneman, D. "Judgment Under Uncertainty: Heuristics and Biases." *Science,* 1974, *185,* 1124–1131.
Tversky, A., and Kahneman, D. "Causal Schemata in Judgments Under Uncertainty." In M. Fishbein (Ed.), *Progress in Social Psychology.* Hillsdale: Erlbaum, 1978.
Ward, W. C., and Jenkins, H. M. "The Display of Information and the Judgment of Contingency." *Canadian Journal of Psychology,* 1965, *19,* 231–241.
Wason, P. C., and Johnson-Laird, P. N. *Psychology of Reasoning.* London: B. T. Batsford, 1972.
Whiting, B. B., and Whiting, J. W. M. *Children of Six Cultures.* Cambridge, Mass.: Harvard University Press, 1975.
Yarrow, M. R., and Waxler, C. Z. "Dimensions and Correlates of Prosocial Behavior in Young Children." *Child Development,* 1976, *47,* 118–125.

Richard A. Shweder is associate professor of human development in the Committee on Human Development, Department of Behavioral Sciences, University of Chicago.

Roy G. D'Andrade is professor of anthropology in the Department of Anthropology, University of California, San Diego.

Social scientists place unwarranted trust in the verbal reports of subjects.

When Are Verbal Reports Veridical?

Donald W. Fiske

Are verbal reports veridical? Such reports are used in a large proportion of social science research and are accepted by investigators all too uncritically. How can we tell when reports are accurate? When they are not accurate, can we estimate the size of the error? The thesis of this chapter is that, a priori, we cannot be sure when verbal reports are veridical, that it is often difficult to establish the veridicality of such reports, and that, under several sets of conditions, reports based on long-term cognitive processes are not veridical. It has become clear that investigators need to examine critically their rationale and evidence for treating verbal reports as veridical and that readers of published research based on such reports must judge the soundness of the investigators' typically unstated rationales.

Social scientists use verbal reports to obtain two major types of information: (1) knowledge acquired by the subject either recently or in the past, knowledge that, at least in principle, can be verified against independent sources of information; (2) information about the subject's internal processes or the products of such processes that cannot be precisely verified against information from any independent source. To obtain verifiable information,

Preparation of this chapter was supported by Grant No. MH 30654 from the National Institute of Mental Health, U.S. Public Health Service. I am indebted to Alan P. Fiske, Susan T. Fiske, Lance Rips, Richard A. Shweder, and Victor Yngve for their valuable comments on an earlier draft of this chapter.

Type 1, investigators use verbal reports, primarily for reasons of economy. But when archival records are available, using verbal reports to save the effort needed to obtain data from those archives is often false economy. Although there may be instances where it is sufficient to obtain verbal answers that approximate the objective facts, such data are liable to systematic bias, both expected and unexpected. For example, Bradburn and Sudman (1979) expected that reports of having voted would be accurate but found they were not. When valid external criteria are available, it should be possible to determine the conditions under which such reports are veridical and perhaps to develop methods for estimating the extent and direction of error where they are not.

The primary emphasis of this chapter is on the major problem of seeking unverifiable information, Type 2, information about internal cognitive activity that is not directly accessible to the investigator by any procedure beyond verbal reporting. In a provocative paper, Nisbett and Wilson (1977b) have provided evidence for an argument that subjects tell more than they really know about their mental processes, that subjects often cannot report accurately on their higher order cognitive functioning. Nisbett and Bellows (1977) assert that subjects gave inaccurate reports about the factors affecting their trait judgments. In a critical reply, Smith and Miller (1978) argue that those authors have overstated the case and that mental processes are accessible and can be reported under some conditions. What are the conditions? Ericsson and Simon (1979, 1980) have made a systematic analysis of the problem and of published evidence in cognitive research. They conclude that, with careful instructions, direct and immediate reporting can be trusted but that less confidence can be placed in reports drawing on long-term memory and requiring intermediate processes involving inference and interpretation. For example, they cite early studies in which subjects could solve problems and form concepts without being able to report verbally the information required to do so.

Ericsson and Simon are concerned primarily with cognitive research. Nisbett and Wilson consider "higher order cognitive processes," including dissonance and attribution research. For instance, they cite their study (Nisbett and Wilson, 1977a) in which the same person's appearance, mannerisms, and accent were rated more favorably when that person acted in a warm manner than when he acted coldly, subjects asserting that it was these presumably constant attributes that produced their degree of overall liking for him. The work of all these authors, together with the research they cite, has implications for the use of verbal reports in other areas of investigation. An investigator using verbal reports must carefully consider the question of their veridicality unless he or she can establish that the warnings of Ericsson and Simon and of Nisbett and Wilson do not apply.

Implicit Trust in Verbal Reports. Verbal reports, oral or written, provide the largest portion of the data used in behavioral science. In the typical instance, the investigator provides instructions, questions, and stimuli and then, at the appropriate time, the subject engages in cognitive processes leading to a report. That description applies to both the procedures used in the cognitive research discussed by Ericsson and Simon and those commonly used elsewhere in behavioral science (in spite of obvious differences between the objectives of the two lines of investigation). Insofar as there is such correspondence, there is a strong likelihood that the cognitive processes are similar for subjects producing verbal reports in the two contexts.

Hence we can pose the question: Do the findings on the veridicality of reports in cognitive research have implications for the veridicality of verbal reports in other areas? The question is important because it is often possible to check veridicality in cognitive work but it is rarely possible elsewhere. Reported perceptions and memories can often be verified consensually: Does the subject perceive a color as green when others call it blue? Does the subject recall correctly his or her mother's birthplace? But external evidence cannot establish that the subject's reports do not correspond with his or her internal experiences: perceptions may be illusory, experiences may be misconstrued, and memories may be distorted or erroneous, and yet the subject *may* be reporting the content of his or her mental processes accurately. (Of course, the subject may, for some reason, make an inaccurate report of those processes.) In practice, an investigator checks on such reports by determining their consistency: Does the subject give the same report when the question is repeated? Does the subject give congruent reports to conceptually related questions? These are, of course, checks on the reliability of the self-reports, and give no assurance about their validity—reliability being a necessary but not sufficient condition for validity.

When using reports on observations of other people, we may be interested in the cognitive processes and the cognitive product of the observer, and here we can use the same kinds of checks to assess consistency. But if, instead of studying observers, we are interested in accurate reports of the behavior of others, we are seeking verifiable information (Type 1) and we require that the observer be consistent with other observers reporting about the same phenomenal events, the same behavior segment of the person being observed. High levels of interobserver agreement can be obtained for judgments about simple actions (Fiske, 1978), especially when the observers are trained intensively (Fiske, 1979). For other types of judgments about people (such as attributive or dispositional), interobserver agreement is usually much lower and the veridicality of the judgments becomes questionable.

For cognitive research using verbal reports, Ericsson and Simon (1980) argue that we need to analyze not only the tasks performed by subjects but also the processes used to produce their verbal responses, that we should have a theory of our measuring instruments. They state that experiments recording verbal responses of any kind need some basic theory about the production of such responses, about the memory storage of the response information, how the response draws on short-term memory, and other relevant matters. Their argument should apply to all verbal reports used as data in behavioral research. Since we are so familiar with questions and answers in everyday living, we have tended to take for granted the use of verbal answers in research.

Intermediate Processing in Verbal Reports

The classification of verbalization procedures in cognitive work presented by Ericsson and Simon (1980) includes a category for reports made after completion of the task-directed processes, reports drawing on long-term memory. Of their subcategories identified by the instructions given, three are pertinent here: reports to general questions, such as how the subjects did the task; reports to questions about hypothetical states, such as how they would react if given the task again; and reports to questions probing general states, questions that the subjects can answer without referring to the experiment itself. Unlike direct reports on what is being attended to, these three kinds of reports require intermediate cognitive processing—such as abstracting and inferring. There is an evident similarity between these three kinds and those used in research on personality, development, and social psychology, as well as in research in other disciplines. Yet the veridicality of exactly those kinds of reports, Ericsson and Simon argue, must be questioned in cognitive research. And if questionable there, must we not consider even more questionable the veridicality of such reports elsewhere? The content of any report is, of course, based on immediate internal experience at the moment of reporting. The basic issue is the correspondence between that content and the prior experiential content sought by the investigator.

Ericsson and Simon point out that dubious reports are produced as a function of the information that the investigator requests, the procedures in questioning, and the process in producing an answer. Regarding the information sought, the investigator may ask about information not attended to, and so the subject uses inference to produce an answer. The investigator may ask why the subject did something, and so the subject must create an interpretation of his or her own behavior—subjects do not ordinarily consider their motives while they are busy adapting to a situation. Again, the question may pertain to information that is not represented in memory in a verbal code or that is not coded in the terms of the question, so that the subject must recode or interpret. More generally, is the information sought by the investigator something that the subject can be expected to remember?

Other problems are noted by Ericsson and Simon. In questioning the subject, the investigator may indicate the information that the investigator expects to find in the verbal report. The investigator may also restrict the response alternatives from which the subject must choose. Again, the questions may generate in the subject background information enabling the subject to give an answer without consulting any memories of cognitive processes. Loftus (1975) has presented very disturbing empirical evidence on the effects of questions with presuppositions, of question wording ("How long . . . " versus "How short . . . ", "frequently" versus "occasionally") and of the range of alternative answers provided.

To produce an answer, the subject must scan to select pertinent information. Retrieval from long-term memory may be incomplete, and of course it may be fallible. The longer the time interval between the event and the reporting, the more likely are deficiencies in the verbal reports. And, as in responding to personality questionnaire items (Kuncel, 1973; Minor and Fiske, 1976), there is much individual variation in the approaches used in the task of responding to the investigator's questions.

Each of these characteristics found in questioning and reporting in cognitive research also appears more or less frequently in survey research, attitude studies, and personality questionnaires. In many investigations where the data are verbal reports, a large number of these features are present. Moreover, the questions in such research often have a less specific referent than in cognitive research, and the referent is commonly more remote in time. For these reasons, the veridicality of reports in these other fields is more difficult to assess; in general, it seems likely to be more questionable.

As a case in point, consider the measurement of values, as Fischhoff, Slovic, and Lichtenstein (in press) have done. Their thesis is that judgments that supposedly reflect people's true values can be substantially affected by subtle aspects of how problems are posed, questions are phrased, and responses are elicited. They note that a person may have no opinion on a matter, or an incoherent opinion, and may or may not realize the fact. They point out that the investigator should use different procedures for finding out "how people express their values," "how people create, revise, and express their opinions," and how they really feel about a value issue." Somewhat similar problems have been noted by Zajonc (1980) in the study of feelings and preferences. He observes that affective reactions may be difficult to verbalize and that there may be affect even without conscious recognition. Both of these points obviously limit the veridicality and hence the utility of verbal reports in this area.

If it is granted that there are potential problems with the veridicality of these several kinds of verbal reports, what are behavioral scientists to do? Necessary but not sufficient are attempts to minimize the possible influence of factors known to increase bias and fallibility, such as demand characteristics (Orne, 1969), experimenter effects (Rosenthal, 1976), and social desirability (Edwards, 1957), to mention just a few. The difficulty for the investigator lies in assuring himself and those reading his papers that he has successfully eliminated or at least minimized these confounding sources of variance. The evidence for adequate controls must come from the particular investigation, but how? Surely not by postexperimental verbal reports from the subjects!

In another approach, ways of assessing veridicality might be sought. Although it might be argued that the methodology of construct validity could be useful here, such methodology seems vulnerable unless the procedures include measurements based on other, quite distinct methods. Convergent validation (Campbell and Fiske, 1959) and convergent operations (Garner, 1974) have value in this context. But if other suitable methods are available, why use verbal reports at all?

Cognitive psychologists frequently use measures that ignore the content of the verbal response, such as response latencies or direction of gaze. But for many research topics, such measures are not suitable and investigators must use verbal reports—for example, to assess verbal learning. Ericsson and Simon contrast the inferential processing required by questioning about a prior experience with the direct report of information being attended to or still in short-term memory. They cite evidence from published literature that supports their argument for the use of such direct reports with minimal time between the event and the report of it. There would seem to be some justification for placing confidence in self-reports of this kind, for example, reports of preference between two immediately present stimuli.

We must conclude that it is not possible a priori to specify exactly the conditions when a verbal report is veridical and when it is not. There is, however, good reason to believe that the likelihood that reports will be veridical increases with the extent to which the report is of more immediate experience and requires a minimum of cognitive processing. This broad generalization does not provide a sufficient basis for choosing one's research method. It seems necessary to establish the veridicality of verbal reports under each set of conditions that the investigator decides to use.

These conclusions pertaining to self-reports have implications for the reports of observers. The recording of observed behavioral acts can be direct and immediate. The initiation and termination of acts can be noted for persons or for animals, either in direct natural observation or from visual recordings. The veridicality of these reports can be determined not only by consensus among observers but also by intensive analyses of recordings replayed at slow speeds (see Duncan and Fiske, 1977).

Reports Taken as Verbal Behavior

Underlying the preceding discussion is an argument that investigators should distinguish between procedures for data-collection and analyses that are independent of the individual subject and procedures that depend upon the active responding of the subject. Whenever we give the subject a task, we must anticipate that the subject will react to aspects of the research activity above and beyond the explicit instructions. We are thus studying research behavior that typically involves producing a response for the investigator, a stage not present in the more naturalistic form of the behavior being studied (see Fiske, 1978, pp. 17–18).

That argument does not, however, rule out the study of verbal reports as verbal behavior, that is, as the responses made to certain questions and other stimuli, ignoring the matter of their correspondence with some inferred events. In applied work, the content of a test item can be ignored while the responses themselves are keyed solely in terms of the extent to which they differentiate two groups of interest (for example, those who succeed in a job and those who fail), the resulting empirical key being applied to responses of future applicants. In basic research, we can determine what words a person produces when asked by a researcher to give a self-description (for example, Turner and Gilliland, 1979). Note, however, that the analysis of such protocols almost invariably requires someone else's cognitive activity to classify each item reported. This second phase of processing the verbal reports also occurs in the use of direct, immediate verbalizations in cognitive research. In both cases, it is fortunate that a permanent record can be made of each report so that the degree of coder agreement on these subsequent activities can be determined and maximized by training.

Although many relevant matters have been omitted here, one assumption must be made explicit. This chapter is concerned with the veridicality, within each verbal report, of each separate element as identified by the investigator for purposes of later analysis. I am convinced that behavioral science cannot advance by using data with major portions of essentially unique determinants or other kinds of "error" of measurement, attempting to compensate for this handicap by pooling an individual's responses to many stimuli (as in personality testing) or by aggregating many persons' responses and dealing with mean responses. Granted that total scores may have high reliability and sizable correlations with other measures, and that differences between group means may generate considerable statistical "confidence," it is doubtful whether a science can be built on relationships of limited magnitude. The basic building block in a science is the single datum. Its quality and veridicality must be maximal.

References

Bradburn, N. M., and Sudman, S. *Improving Interview Method and Questionnaire Design: Response Effects to Threatening Questions in Survey Research.* San Francisco: Jossey-Bass, 1979.

Campbell, D. T., and Fiske, D. W. "Convergent and Discriminant Validation by the Multitrait-Multimethod Matrix." *Psychological Bulletin,* 1959, *56,* 81–105.

Duncan, S., Jr., and Fiske, D. W. *Face-to-Face Interaction: Research, Methods, and Theory.* Hillsdale, N.J.: Erlbaum, 1977.

Edwards, A. L. *The Social Desirability Variable in Personality Assessment and Research.* New York: Dryden, 1957.

Ericsson, K. A., and Simon, H. H. "Thinking-Aloud Protocols as Data: Effects of Verbalization." Department of Psychology, Carnegie-Mellon University. C. I. P. Working Paper No. 397, March 25, 1979.

Ericsson, K. A., and Simon, H. H. "Verbal Reports as Data." *Psychological Review,* 1980, *87,* 215–251.

Fischhoff, B., Slovic, P., and Lichtenstein, S. "Knowing What You Want: Measuring Labile Values." In T. Wallsten (Ed.), *Cognitive Processes in Choice and Decision Behavior.* Hillsdale, N.J.: Erlbaum, in press.

Fiske, D. W. *Strategies for Personality Research: The Observation Versus Interpretation of Behavior.* San Francisco: Jossey-Bass, 1978.

Fiske, D. W. "A Demonstration of the Value of Interchangeable Observers." *Journal of Behavioral Assessment,* 1979, *51,* 251–258.

Garner, W. R. *The Processing of Information and Structure.* Hillsdale, N.J.: Erlbaum, 1974.

Kuncel, R. B. "Response Processes and Relative Location of Subject and Item." *Educational and Psychological Measurement,* 1973, *33,* 545–563.

Loftus, E. F. "Leading Questions and the Eyewitness Report." *Cognitive Psychology,* 1975, *7,* 560–572.

Minor, M. J., and Fiske, D. W. "Response Processes During the Description of Others." *Educational and Psychological Measurement,* 1976, *36,* 829–833.
Nisbett, R. E., and Bellows, N. "Verbal Reports About Causal Influences on Social Judgments." *Journal of Personality and Social Psychology,* 1977, *35,* 613–624.
Nisbett, R. E., and Wilson, T. D. "The Halo Effect: Evidence for Unconscious Alteration of Judgment." *Journal of Personality and Social Psychology,* 1977a, *35,* 250–256.
Nisbett, R. E., and Wilson, T. D. "Telling More Than We Can Know: Verbal Reports on Mental Processes." *Psychological Review,* 1977b, *84,* 231–259.
Orne, M. T. "Demand Characteristics and the Concept of Quasi-Controls." In R. Rosenthal and R. L. Rosnow (Eds.), *Artifact in Behavioral Research.* New York: Academic Press, 1969.
Rosenthal, R. *Experimenter Effects in Behavioral Research.* (Rev. ed.) New York: Irvington, 1976.
Smith, E. R., and Miller, F. D. "Limits on Perceptions of Cognitive Processes: A Reply to Nisbett and Wilson." *Psychological Review,* 1978, *85,* 355–362.
Turner, R. G., and Gilliland, L. "The Comparative Relevance and Predictive Validity of Subject Generated Trait Descriptions." *Journal of Personality,* 1979, *47,* 230–244.
Zajonc, R. B. "Feeling and Thinking: Preferences Need No Inferences." *American Psychologist,* 1980, *35,* 151–175.

Donald W. Fiske is professor of psychology and chair, Committee on Methodology of Behavioral Research, Department of Behavioral Sciences, University of Chicago.

Decisions derived from simple algorithms and a few explicit principles work better than intuitive judgments.

You Can't Systematize Human Judgment: Dyslexia

Robyn M. Dawes

Friends tell me that important human judgment is often ineffable, unsystematic, and intuitive.

I agree. And it is, therefore, often bad.

Friends tell me that decisions that are effable, systematic, and explicit are dehumanized decisions.

I agree. But they are "dehumanized" only for the decision maker, and I am concerned with the consequences for the people affected by the decisions. Bad decisions are dehumanizing for them.

Friends tell me that judgments about people must be holistic, because people can be understood and appreciated only as integrated, indivisible entities.

I agree, if the characteristic of the person to be judged is a gestalt (such as beauty). If it is not (for instance, academic or work potential), then a holistic judgment is simply a delusion.

Friends tell me that they are good judges—particularly of people—when they make holistic, ineffable, intuitive, and unsystematic judgments.

I would like to thank Frank Steck for sending me the article about Duke University, and Richard Nisbett and Myron Rothbart for their valuable comments on an earlier draft of this chapter.

I agree only that they think they are good judges. Most well-adjusted people believe that they make good decisions; judgmental successes are remembered more readily than are judgmental failures, and the role of extraneous factors is more readily appreciated in accounting for failures than for successes.

Friends tell me that effable and systematic decisions might be computerized, thereby bringing us closer to 1984 and the establishment of a Kafkaesque bureaucracy. I agree that 1984 is four years away. The essence of a Kafkaesque bureaucracy, however, is not that it has rules; rather it is that it appears to have coherent or humane rules but does not. ("What must I do to get out of the hospital?" "You know the answer to that." Or, "Your comprehensive homeowners policy covered your house only on its present foundations; but the mud slide moved it two inches off its foundation before totally demolishing it . . .") And computers can be used either for or against people; for example, I have yet to hear anyone complain about the airlines' use of computers—which makes booking, connecting, and rerouting pleasant and efficient. Or complain about the use of computers in successfully irradiating tumors.

The central thesis of this chapter is that in a wide variety of psychological contexts, systematic decisions based on a few explicable and defensible principles are superior to intuitive decisions—because they work better, because they are not subject to conscious or unconscious biases on the part of the decision maker, because they can be explicated and debated, and because their basis can be understood by those most affected by them.

Decisions About Admission

The major decision I will discuss is that of admitting students to academic institutions. First, I will present descriptions about how it is actually done; second, I will present theory and research evidence indicating how it might be done better; third, I will discuss the ethical implications of doing it better—including those for affirmative action programs; finally I will recount how graduate students are chosen at the University of Oregon.

How are such decisions usually made? Two articles appeared in the spring of 1979 describing undergraduate admissions procedures at two leading universities, Brown and Duke. I will excerpt these in a nonrandom, biased, and unsystematic manner in order to show how such decisions are typically made.

A Session at Brown*

On a rainy Sunday morning in March, Brown Admissions Director Jim Rogers and three members of the admissions committee contemplate a fat

*Thomas, 1979, pp. 51–52. Reprinted by permission from TIME, the Weekly Newsmagazine; © Time Inc., 1979.

computer printout. It measures, in code, the credentials of the 11,421 high school seniors who have applied to Brown. Next to each applicant's name, a long string of numbers and cryptic abbreviations shows college board scores, class rank, grade-point average, and a preliminary rating for academic promise and personal quality [?] on a scale of 1 to 6. Other symbols reveal more: "LEG 1" is a legacy, the son of a Brown alumnus. "M1" is a black; "M8" a Chicano. "50" means the Brown football coach is interested, "70" that Brown's development office has marked the candidate's parents as potential benefactors.

The committee passes around a thick application folder from "Mary." "Whoops," says Rogers. "A 'Pinocchio'!" In Brown admissions jargon, that means her guidance counselor has checked off boxes rating her excellent for academic ability but only good or average for humor, imagination, and character. On the printed recommendation form, the low checks stick out from the high ones like a long, thin nose. A Pinocchio is often fatal. "A rating of average usually means the guidance counselor thinks there is something seriously wrong," explains Admissions Officer Paulo de Oliveira. Mary's interview with a Brown alumnus was also lukewarm, and worse, she has written a "jock essay" (a very short one). Rogers scrawls a Z, the code for rejection, on her folder.

The next morning the admissions committee scans applications from a small rural high school in the Southwest. It is searching for prized specimens known as "neat small-town kids." Amy is near the top of her class, with mid-500 verbals, high-600 math and science. She is also poor, white, and "geo"—she would add to the geographic and economic diversity that saves Brown from becoming a postgraduate New England prep school. While just over 20 percent of the New York State applicants will get in, almost 40 percent will be admitted from Region 7—Oklahoma, Texas, Arkansas, and Louisiana. Amy's high school loves her, and she wants to study engineering. Brown badly wants engineering students; unfortunately, Amy spells engineering wrong. "Dyslexia," says Jimmy Wrenn, a linguistics professor. After some debate, the committee puts her on the waiting list.

A Session at Duke*

It is a sunlit Thursday morning, and around a long wooden table a college admissions committee squints at thick books of computer printouts and argues about a black high school senior with much promise but bad grades.

One of twelve children from a Detroit ghetto family, he wants to attend Duke University here, but his case perplexes admissions officials. Although they want to admit more blacks, this young man ranks in the bottom fifth of his class, and his scores are just average on the Scholastic Aptitude Test, which is said to measure college potential. "He's scary," mutters Edward Lingenheld, Duke's admissions director. Yet the Massachusetts prep school that the stu-

*Reprinted by permission of Anthony Ramirez, *Cream of the Crop,* © Dow Jones & Co., Inc., 1979, all rights reserved.

dent is attending on an affirmative-action scholarship is one of the best private schools in the country. It backs him strongly, saying his character and leadership ability are outstanding.

After a few minutes of sharp debate, the committee, swayed mainly by the school's praise, decides to accept him. He is one of more than 6,800 high school seniors who want to get into Duke's freshman class next fall. Only 1,000 will make it.

Watching the admissions committee's deliberations here at Duke for a few days shows the shifting and sorting that lands some students in the college of their choice, and leaves others—often with almost identical grades and test scores—rejected.

The admissions marathon begins in early December, when the first applications trickle in. In all, the staff must ponder more than 8,000 applications (counting an extra 1,200 for the engineering and nursing schools), most of them in about nine weeks. Even with the hiring of seven part-timers (mostly faculty wives) to evaluate applications, each permanent staffer must study thoroughly as many as fifty applications a day.

The fatigue is evident. "I want to know if I goofed," says David Belton, an admissions staffer, asking advice from other staffers about a candidate. He says he had only two hours' sleep when he read the applicant's folder. (The candidate, after review, stays rejected.)

A major quality the committee looks for is "spark."

One student, typical of many, seems to lack it. The son of a prosperous Harvard graduate, he is trying to decide where he's going in life. For "anticipated career" and "anticipated major" he has checked "undecided." Gifted in mathematics (a 790 on a math section of the S.A.T.), he is only a B student overall.

The committee considers his extracurricular activities lackluster. He is a stamp collector, a Boy Scout, and a Sunday school teacher, who also plays the piano and guitar and sings. On Duke's scale, his grades and extracurricular activities rank him a "D/D."

Nevertheless, an admissions staffer includes a note in the student's folder: "Bad Soph year but super scores. I really like him. Fine student—admit if possible."

His high school also recommends him "with enthusiasm," but an admissions staffer who interviewed him notes his "lethargic demeanor." David Miller, another staffer, says his admission would be "tantamount to saying scores can get you in."

The student writes, "Years from now, all the pressure of this decision will probably seem funny. But right now it seems very important to get it all sorted out. I will be relieved when the work and the waiting are over and commitment has been made, for better or worse."

The committee rejects him.

As I learned when selecting graduate students at the University of Oregon, such selection procedures are exciting, fun. Few things beat the combination of exhilaration and exhaustion felt by those in a compatible group faced with a demanding mission. The atmosphere in admissions committees is often that of a benign war room; crucial decisions are made about others' lives, but no one gets killed. It is not, however, so much fun for the Pinocchios of this world—or for those of us who cannot spell too well.

Clinical Versus Statistical Prediction

Does it work? That is, are decisions made in this manner more efficacious than those made by a dull and systematic statistical integration of the predictive information at hand? This question has been studied extensively by psychologists and others interested in such outcomes as college success (Sarbin, 1943), graduate school success (Dawes, 1971), parole violation (Burgess, 1941), and psychiatric diagnosis (Goldberg, 1965). In all these studies, the same basic information presented to a clinician or clinicians asked to make an intuitive ("clinical") prediction was also used in a statistical model predicting that same outcome. This information usually consisted of test scores or biographical facts, but occasionally included observer ratings of specific attributes as well. In 1954, Meehl published an influential book in which he summarized approximately twenty such studies comparing the clinical integration method with the statistical one. In all studies, the statistical method did better, or the two methods tied. In most of these studies, the statistical method of choice was a regression equation—that is, a simple weighted average of the appropriately coded information where the weights are chosen in such a way as to maximize predictability. (The usual criterion of evaluating the models was the multiple correlation coefficient computed between predicted and obtained outcomes; in all cases, these correlation coefficients were computed on a "cross-validation sample," one independent of that from which the weights were obtained.)

Approximately ten years later, Sawyer (1966) reviewed a total of forty-five studies comparing clinical and statistical prediction. There was again *no* study in which a clinical combination method was superior to what Sawyer termed a "mechanical" (statistical) one, and in a majority of studies, the statistical prediction was superior. Unlike Meehl, Sawyer did not limit his review to situations where the clinical judge had information identical to that on which the statistical model was based, and he even included two studies (Bloom and Brundage, 1947; Schiedt, 1936) where the clinical judge had access to *more* information (an interview) and yet did *worse*. (The near total lack of validity of unstructured interviews as predictive techniques is documented and discussed in an article by Kelly in 1954, one that has to my knowledge gone unchallenged since.)

Nothing published in the standard journals after Sawyer's review has demonstrated that a context exists in which clinical prediction is superior. On the other hand, the number of contexts in which statistical prediction has been shown to be superior has grown consistently (Dawes, 1979)—some of the more interesting being prediction of longevity of patients with Hodgkins Disease (Einhorn, 1972) and prediction of business failures (Libby, 1976).

Why do regression equations do so well compared to clinical judgment? First, it should be pointed out that neither method does as well as many people would like (comparisons typically being among multiple correlation coefficients ranging from .25 to .60). That has led many critics to dismiss the superiority of the statistical predictions on the grounds that "twice nothing is nothing" (letter from a dean quoted in Dawes, 1976a, pp. 6–7). But as I have argued elsewhere (Dawes, 1979) such criticisms are based on the assumption that the criteria to be predicted *should* be highly predictable, and there is no basis for such an assumption other than the reassuring hope that life is in fact predictable. (It is not.) Nor is there reason to believe that other experts making clinical predictions would do better than did those studied—although the argument that the wrong clinicians were used persists among many of my colleagues, who modestly maintain that *really* well-trained and insightful clinicians like themselves would not be subject to the biases, pitfalls, or incapacities of others.

So the regression equations do well compared to clinical judgment—perhaps as well as can be expected. The reason is that, in the contexts studied, each variable used in the prediction can easily be coded to have a *conditionally monotonic* relationship to the criterion. That is, higher values on each predictor are associated with higher values on the criterion irrespective of the values on the other predictors. For example, students with higher undergraduate grade point averages (GPA's) have a higher probability of success in graduate school than do those with lower GPA's; students with higher Graduate Record Examination scores (GRE's) have a higher probability of success than do those with lower GRE's, and there is no "crossed" ("disordinal") interaction that leads the GPA probability of success prediction to reverse direction at certain levels of GRE scores, or *vice versa.* Given that "more is better"—that is, given conditional monotonicity in the predictive situation—*regression equations do an extremely good job of making the prediction.* Dawes and Corrigan (1974) have summarized empirical, simulation, and mathematical studies all demonstrating the general principle that even when the best prediction of the criterion is not a weighted average of prediction variables, this average obtained from constructing a regression equation yields predictions that are excellent approximations to the best ones—provided only that the relationship is conditionally monotonic. So the regression equations work.

Even if a variable does not have a monotonic relationship with the criterion, in most contexts it is possible to rescale it so that it does. For example, if we were evaluating applicants for jobs in which too much intelligence were as detrimental as too little (such as custodian), then we could easily define a new variable termed "intellectual mediocrity" that would be assessed in terms of distance from an ideal level of mediocre capacity. All such "single peaked" functions can easily be converted to monotonic ones by defining desirability as distance from the peak (ideal level). (The reader is invited to think for a moment about variables that might be useful in predicting such phenomena as academic success, heart attacks, job success, longevity, or bankruptcy—to see how most are conditionally monotonic to begin with, and how the remainder can easily be made so.) In fact, almost all psychological, medical, or finan cial variables we use to predict outcomes of interest are monotone, or sin· gle peaked, and do not interact. No matter how much some of us may wish to get around it, it is better to be smarter, stronger, and more beautiful—have blood pressure nearer to 120/80, be closer to age 29, and be moderately aggressive.)

Why are clinical judges not so good at the information integration process? Studies from experimental psychology have shown that people are very poor at integrating information from different dimensions if these are inherently noncomparable—as, for example, are a grade point average and a test score. There is even evidence that people cannot keep two distinct "analyzable" dimensions in mind at the same time (Shepard, 1964), especially if they are asked to make judgments in which information about one of these two dimensions may be missing (Slovic and MacPhillamy, 1974). If the cognitive processes of admissions committee members are not different qualitatively from those of experimental subjects, then it is not surprising that such judges do not integrate information well.

But clinical judges are important. The statistical model may integrate the information in an optimal manner, but it is always the individual (judge, clinician) who chooses the variables. Moreover, it is the human judge who knows the directional relationship between the predictor variables and the criterion of interest, or who can code the variables in such a way that they have a clear directional relationship. And it is precisely in situations where the predictor variables are good and where they have a monotonic relationship with the criterion that regression equations work well.

Weighting the Variables. The admissions committee or single clinical judge often does not have a regression equation available. The determination of the optimal weights used in such an equation requires a careful study of a large number of individual cases sampled from the population of people or objects to be judged—or the estimation of the weights may be severely in error. If such a study is impossible, can nothing be done other than to fall back on inferior clinical intuition in lieu of a superior but nonexistent regression equation? The answer is no. In the last five years, there has been a resurgence of interest in the degree to which weights that are not optimal may yield results close to the optimal ones. Dawes and Corrigan (1974) showed that weights *randomly* chosen—but in the right direction—yield results that are close to those that are obtained from optimal weights. (In those studies, all variables were made statistically comparable by standardizing them.) Moreover, in five judgment contexts, the outcomes obtained from pseudo-regression equations devised from such weights on the average outperformed clinical judges making the same predictions. Finally, Dawes and Corrigan showed that unit weights (+1 if the variable has a positive relationship with the criterion, −1 otherwise) did better on the average than did random weights, and did *much* better than did the clinical judges. Dawes and Corrigan concluded that (1974, p. 195) "the whole trick is to know what variables to look at and then to know how to add."

Later, the degree to which changes in predictions are affected by changes in weights (provided changes in signs are not involved) has been investigated by Edwards (1978), Einhorn and Hogarth (1975), Gardiner and Edwards (1975), Green (1977), Wainer (1976), and Wainer and Thissen (1976). These investigators have all reached the same conclusion: the changes in prediction are affected very little—not enough to make any difference in most applied situations.

Implementation of the Dawes-Corrigan trick of using experts to select the variables and then simply adding their values appears to "dehumanize" prediction situations—particularly those in which people are being selected or rejected. People are reduced to "mere numbers," and the allocation of scarce social resources is made on the basis of these numbers. So, even if such a procedure works better than does clinical judgment, should we not discard it? Is it not "horribly unfair to reject people without even interviewing them?" as I overheard one rejected applicant to Santa Barbara complain at the Los Angeles Renaissance Fair last summer. "How can they possibly tell what I'm like?"

The answer is that they cannot—nor could they with an interview (or a Rorschach test). The selection system is meant to do the *best possible* job of allocating scarce positions in graduate school; it will make mistakes (just as clinical judgment does), but fewer. Some people who will be rejected without an interview *will* have more potential than some of those accepted without one, but the research indicates that interviews will not discover which ones. Moreover, performance on an interview is *not* as meritorious a characteristic as a mere number like an undergraduate record—which represents work over three and a half years in a minimum of thirty-six classes. The rejected applicant who complained implied that she would rather be judged on the basis of a half hour talk under unusual circumstances (she is trying to impress an interviewer of unknown predilections and biases) than be judged on her past history of work and accomplishment. Unless that history is deficient, she might opt for the mere number; at the very least, if she wished each individual social decision to be made as if it were a general policy (Rawls, 1958) she would do so. (For a discussion of the ethics of allocating scarce resources on the basis of a systematic weighting of a few predictive and meritorious variables, see Dawes, 1977.)

I do not mean to imply that interviews are never useful. First, a structured interview or situation is of use if it taps a behavior that is important in the situation for which the interviewee is being considered; for example, job applicants for academic positions are routinely asked to give a talk about their work; the clarity, charm, and enthusiasm with which they can lecture—in particular about their own work—are important factors in determining how highly they will be evaluated in an academic position were they to obtain one. (I am not arguing that it is moral or socially productive that university professors be evaluated on such factors—just that they are.) Second, an unstructured interview may allow the interviewer to assess how he or she responds to the interviewee. Affective responses in particular are often formed precipitously and cannot be explained by a *conscious* weighting of components (Zajonc, 1980; Posner, personal communication). If it is important to assess such reactions—for instance, if the interviewee is applying to be a secretary of the interviewer—then clearly an interview is appropriate. But in the situations described in this chapter, the interview is neither structured to contain a sample of relevant work, nor is it conducted by a person who will have a close supervisory relationship to the applicant. The systematic combination of relevant predictors is superior.

Discrimination? Does this select-and-average-relevant-variables system tend to exclude minority applicants? Not unless it is implemented stupidly. It is true that minority applicants tend to score lower than majority ones on most selection variables. But that only demonstrates the *need* for affirmative action. It certainly does not demonstrate that such applicants are dumber in any biological sense, nor that the *tests* are somehow biased against minority group members. The reason for these conclusions is that the tests do exactly what they were constructed to do—assess potential for performance in a predominantly white middle class culture, and there is no such thing as aptitude independent of experience (certain naive ideas about mental functioning being different from all other functioning notwithstanding). Since on the whole minority applicants have less experience in this culture than do majority group applicants, their aptitude scores are lower.

What to do? Consistent with the approach advocated in this chapter, I would simply add a factor with an explicit score for minority group status. This factor would be sufficiently large to guarantee that *on the average* (not as part of a quota for each year) the desired proportion of minority group members would be selected. Only the most qualified minority applicants would be admitted, while only the least qualified majority students who would otherwise be admitted would be rejected. Moreover, the predictability of the selection criteria would be affected very little (Dawes, 1976b), even if the minority group applicants did as poorly on the whole on the criterion behavior as on the standard selection variables. (A similar approach was first proposed by Darlington, 1971).

Is that legal? In the Bakke decision (McCormack, 1978), Justice Powell—who held the pivotal vote—stated that ethnic origin may be a factor in admissions to academic institutions. But there appear to be three qualifications. First, the "purpose" must be to have a representative student body rather than to affect society. (I guess I just cannot think like a lawyer; to me, identical outcomes imply the same policy.) Second, he implied—although he did not state—that an ethnic origin factor must be one of many, such as ability to play left guard. Third, he prohibited "doctoring" test scores for ethnic origin, although the ethnicity factor may be added later. (Again, believing that the sum of sums is equal to the sum of sums, I fail to see the distinction between first adding something to a test score and then amalgamating the result with other things—as opposed to amalgamating the test score with other things and then adding an ethnicity factor.) The answer to the question at the beginning of this paragraph is: Maybe.

How would the type of procedure advocated here be implemented? Recently, Goldberg (1977) has described the admissions procedure for evaluating students who have applied to the graduate program in psychology at the University of Oregon. First, each applicant's past record and aptitude test scores are amalgamated in a simple additive combination:

$$\mathrm{GPA} + \frac{\mathrm{V} + \mathrm{Q}}{200}$$

where GPA is the undergraduate grade point average, and V and Q are raw scores on the verbal and quantitative parts of the GRE respectively. Note that this formula is *compensatory;* applicants with mediocre records may score high if they show evidence of outstanding aptitude, and vice versa. (In fact, even the verbal and quantitative parts of the GRE are compensatory.)

Majority applicants who score below 9.7 are rejected. Past research (Dawes, 1971) has shown that such applicants stand no chance of being admitted even when purely intuitive decisions are made. The use of this formula—and its publication—saves both heartache for students who have no chance of being admitted, and faculty time and guilt in rejecting huge numbers of such applicants.

Finally, only the majority students passing the 9.7 cut and all minority students are considered on a case-by-case basis. Here, letters of recommendation are important, but unfortunately no way of coding them to make them comparable has yet been devised. What the reviewers look for is concrete evidence of accomplishment (such as independent research projects). Unfortunately, in my view, the reviewers also look for "fit" between the student's interests and theirs. (It seems pretty silly to me for Duke to reject a 17-year-old applicant partly because he is honestly "undecided" about his major. In fact, one could argue that many applicants who have decided on a career at age 17 are suffering from "premature closure" of the intellect—or premature maturity in general. Similarly, college seniors who claim to know the interests they wish to pursue in psychology for the next forty-five years may well include those with the least inquiring and flexible minds. Ditto for those rated as "mature" by the letter writers. That is all speculation. No studies. In the absence of any evidence that such interest variables are predictive—and they are certainly not meritorious—I would ignore them.)

This procedure is dry, unexciting, "peripheralistic," routinized (hence effable), and communicable. Basically, Oregon weights three factors: how well the applicant has done in the past, how intelligent he or she appears to be on the basis of a standardized test, and what independent work he or she has done of the type that will be expected in graduate school and beyond. The Oregon psychologists do not claim to understand applicants in their entirety; in fact, they do not even claim to have "spark" detectors in their heads. Perhaps they are less able than are the admissions officers elsewhere who search for spark. Or perhaps, being familiar with the literature on the poor track records of such clinical judgments, the Oregon psychologists are merely a bit more modest. At any rate, the applicants to Oregon are chosen on the basis of what they *do,* not on the basis of how they impress. *And they know how they will be chosen.* While the type of approach used at Oregon has been decried by some psychologists (Holt, 1978) as failing to be "centralist" and "dynamic" (and everyone knows that the center is better than the periphery, and that dynamism is better than stagnation), it has two rather compelling things going for it. (1) It judges people on the basis of what they do (and how else should people be judged?) (2) It works.

References

Bloom, R. F., and Brundage, E. G. "Prediction of Success in Elementary Schools for Enlisted Personnel." In D. B. Stuit (Ed.), *Personal Research and Test Development in the Bureau of Naval Personnel.* Princeton, N.J.: Princeton University Press, 1947.

Burgess, E. W. "An Experiment in the Standardization of the Case-Study Method." *Sociometry,* 1941, *4,* 329-348.

Darlington, R. B. "Another Look at Cultural Fairness." *Journal of Educational Measurement.* 1971, *3* (2), 71-82.

Dawes, R. M. "A Case Study of Graduate Admissions: Application of Three Principles of Human Decision-Making." *American Psychologist,* 1971, *26,* 181-188.

Dawes, R. M. "Shallow Psychology." In J. Carroll and J. Payne (Eds.), *Cognition and Social Behavior.* Hillsdale, N.J.: Erlbaum, 1976a.

Dawes, R. M. "Multivariate Selection of Students in a Racist Society: A Systematically Unfair Approach." In M. Zelany (Ed.), *Multiple Criteria Decision Making: Kyoto 1975.* New York: Springer Verlag, 1976b.

Dawes, R. M. "Case-by-Case Versus Rule-Generated Procedures for the Allocation of Scarce Resources." In M. F. Kaplan and S. Schwartz (Eds.), *Human Judgment and Decision Processes: Applications in an Applied Setting.* New York: Springer Verlag, 1977.

Dawes, R. M. "The Robust Beauty of Improper Linear Models." *American Psychologist,* 1979, *34,* 571-582.

Dawes, R. M., and Corrigan, B. "Linear Models in Decision Making." *Psychological Bulletin,* 1974, *81,* 95-106.

Edwards, W. M. "Technology for Director Dubious: Evaluation and Discussion in Public Contexts." In K. R. Hammond (Ed.), *Judgment and Decision in Public Policy Formation.* Boulder, Colo.: Westview Press, 1978.

Einhorn, H. J. "Expert Measurement and Mechanical Combination." *Organizational Behavior and Human Performance,* 1972, *7,* 86-106.

Einhorn, H. J., and Hogarth, R. M. "Unit Weighting Schemes for Decision Making." *Organizational Behavior and Human Performance,* 1975, *13,* 171-192.

Gardiner, P. C., and Edwards, W. "Public Values: Multiattribute—Utility Measurement for Social Decision Making." In M. F. Kaplan and S. Schwartz (Eds.), *Human Judgment and Decision Processes.* New York: Academic Press, 1975.

Goldberg, L. R. "Diagnostician Versus Diagnostic Signs: The Diagnosis of Psychosis Versus Neurosis from the MMPI." *Psychological Monographs,* 1965, 79 (*9,* whole No. 602).

Goldberg, L. R. "Admissions to the Ph.D. Program in the Department of Psychology." *American Psychologist,* 1977, *32,* 663-668.

Green, B. F., Jr. "Parameter Sensitivity in Multivariate Methods." *Multivariate Behavioral Research,* 1977, *12,* 263-287.

Holt, R. R. *Methods in Clinical Psychology.* Vol. 2: *Prediction and Research.* New York: Plenum Press, 1978.

Kelley, E. L. "Evaluation of the Interview as a Selection Technique." In *Proceedings of the 1953 International Conference on Testing Problems.* Princeton, N.J.: Educational Testing Service, 1954.

Libby, R. "Man Versus Model of Man: Some Conflicting Evidence." *Organizational Behavior and Human Performance,* 1976, *16,* 1–12.

Liebert, L. "How Stanford Chooses Who Gets It." *San Francisco Chronicle,* April 30, 1979, p. 1.

McCormack, W. "The Bakke Decision: Implications for Higher Education Admissions." A report of the ACE-AALS Committee on Education, American Council on Education, Association of American Law Schools, 1978.

Meehl, P. E. *Clinical Versus Statistical Prediction: A Theoretical Analysis and Review of the Literature.* Minneapolis: University of Minnesota Press, 1954.

Ramirez, A. "Cream of the Crop?" *The Wall Street Journal,* April 6, 1979, *193* (68), p.1.

Rawls, J. "Justice as Fairness." *Philosophical Review,* 1958, *67,* 164–194.

Sarbin, T. R. "A Contribution to the Study of Actuarial and Individual Methods of Prediction." *American Journal of Sociology,* 1943, *48,* 593–602.

Sawyer, J. "Measurement *and* Prediction, Clinical *and* Statistical." *Psychological Bulletin,* 1966, *66,* 178–200.

Schiedt, R. *"Ein Beitrag zum Problem der Rückfallsprognose."* (Doctoral dissertation.) Munich: Müncher Zeitungs Verlag, 1936.

Shepard, R. N. "On Subjectively Optimal Selection Among Multi-Attribute Alternatives." In M. W. Shelley, and G. L. Bryan (Eds.), *Human Judgments and Optimality.* New York: Wiley, 1964.

Slovic, P., and MacPhillamy, D. J. "Dimensional Commensurability and Cue Utilization in Comparative Judgment." *Organizational Behavior and Human Performance,* 1974, *11,* 172–194.

Thomas, E. "Choosing the Class of '83." *Time,* April 9, 1979, pp. 51–52.

Wainer, H. "Estimating Coefficients in Linear Models: It Don't Make No Nevermind." *Psychological Bulletin,* 1976, *83,* 312–317.

Wainer, H., and Thissen, D. "Three Steps Toward Robust Regression." *Psychometrica,* 1976, *41,* 9–34.

Zajonc, R. B. "Feeling and Thinking: Preferences Need No Inferences." *American Psychologist,* 1980, *35,* 151–175.

Robyn M. Dawes is professor and head, Department of Psychology, University of Oregon, and consultant at Decision Research, 1201 Oak Street, Eugene, Oregon 97401.

Learning from the past looks easy, but there are a thousand pitfalls.

For Those Condemned to Study the Past: Reflections on Historical Judgment

Baruch Fischhoff

"I often think it odd that history should be so dull, for a great deal of it must be invention."
—Catherine Morlund

Benson (1972) has identified four reasons for studying the past: to entertain, to create a group (or national) identity, to reveal the extent of human possibility, and to develop systematic knowledge about our world, knowledge that may eventually improve our ability to predict and control. On a conscious level, at least, we behavioral scientists restrict ourselves to the last motive. In its pursuit, we do case studies, program evaluations, and literature reviews. We even conduct experiments, creating artificial histories upon which we can perform our post mortems.

Three basic questions seem to arise in our retrospections: (1) Are there patterns upon which we can capitalize so as to make ourselves wiser in the

My thanks to Lita Furby, Lewis Goldberg, Sarah Lichtenstein, and Paul Slovic for their perceptive comments on earlier drafts.

future? (2) Are there instances of folly in which we can identify mistakes to avoid? (3) Are we really condemned to repeat the past if we do not study it? That is, do we really learn anything by looking backward?

Whatever the question we are asking, it is generally assumed that the past will readily reveal the answers it holds. Of hindsight and foresight, the latter appears as the more troublesome perspective. One can explain and understand any old event if an appropriate effort is applied. Prediction, however, is acknowledged to be rather more tricky. The present essay investigates this presumption by taking a closer look at some archetypal attempts to tap the past. Perhaps its most general conclusion is that we should hold the past in a little more respect when we attempt to plumb its secrets. While the past entertains, ennobles, and expands quite readily, it enlightens only with delicate coaxing.

Looking for Wisdom

Formal Modeling. While the past never repeats itself in dctail, it is often viewed as having repetitive elements. People make the same kinds of decisions, face the same kinds of challenges, and suffer the same kinds of misfortune often enough for behavioral scientists to believe that they can detect recurrent patterns. Such faith prompts psychometricians to study the diagnostic secrets of ace clinicians, clinicians to look for correlates of aberrant behavior, brokers to hunt for harbingers of price increases, and dictators to ponder revolutionary situations. Their search usually has a logic paralleling that of multiple regression or correlation. A set of relevant cases is collected and each member is characterized on a variety of dimensions. The resulting matrix is scoured for significant relationships that might aid us in predicting the future.

The Daily Racing Form, for example, offers the earnest handicapper some one hundred pieces of information on each horse in any given race. The handicapper with a flair for data processing might commit to some computer's memory the contents of a bound volume of the *Form* and try to derive a formula predicting speed as a weighted sum of scores on various dimensions. For example:

$$\tilde{y} = b_1x_1 + b_2x_2 + b_3x_3 \qquad (1)$$

where $\tilde{y}$ is our best guess at a horse's speed, x_1 is its percentage of victories in previous races, x_2 is its jockey's percentage of winning races, and x_3 is the weight it will carry in the present race. When scores are standardized (by subtracting the mean and then dividing by the standard deviation), the b_i reflect the importance of the different factors. If $b_1 = 2b_2$, then a given change in the horse's percentage of wins affects our speed prediction twice as much as an equivalent change in jockey's percentage, because past performances have proved twice as sensitive to x_1 as to x_2.

Sounds easy, but there are a thousand pitfalls. One emerges when the predictors (x_i) are correlated, as might (and in fact does) happen were winning horses to draw winning jockeys or vice versa. In such cases of multicollinearity, each variable has some independent ability to explain past performance and the two have some shared ability. When the weights are determined, that shared explanatory capacity will somehow be split between the two. Typically, that split renders the weights (b_i) uninterpretable with any degree of precision. Thus the regression equation cannot be treated as a theory of horse racing, showing the importance of various factors.

A more modest theoretical goal would simply be to determine which factors are and which factors are not important, on the basis of how much each adds to our understanding of y. The logic here is that of stepwise regression; additional variables are added to the equation as long as they add something to its overall predictive (or explanatory) power. Yet even this minimalistic strategy can run afoul of multicollinearity. If many reflections of a particular factor (such as different aspects of breeding) are included, their shared explanatory ability may be divided up into such small pieces that no one aspect makes a "significant" contribution.

Of course, these nuances may be of relatively little interest to handicappers as long as the formula works well enough to help them somewhat in beating the odds. We scientist types, however, want wisdom as well as efficacy from our techniques. It is hard for us to give up interpreting weights. Regression procedures not only express, but also produce, understanding (or, at least, results) in a mechanical, repeatable fashion. Small wonder then that they have been pursued doggedly despite their limitations.

One of the best documented pursuits has been in the study of clinical judgment. Clinical judgment is exercised by a radiologist who sorts X-rays of ulcers into "benign" and "malignant," by a personnel officer who chooses the best applicants from a set of candidates, or by a crisis center counselor who decides which callers threatening suicide are serious. In each of these examples, the diagnosis involves making a decision on the basis of a set of cues or attributes. When, as in these examples, the decision is repetitive and all cases can be characterized by the same cue, it is possible to model the judge's decision-making policy statistically. One collects a set of cases for which the expert has made a summary judgment (benign, serious) and then derives a regression equation, like (1), whose weights show the importance the judge has assigned to each cue.

Two decades of such policy-capturing studies persistently produced a disturbing pair of conclusions: (1) simple linear models, using a weighted sum of the cues, did an excellent job of postdicting judges' decisions, although (2) the judges claimed that they were using much more complicated strategies (Goldberg, 1968, 1970; Slovic and Lichtenstein, 1971). A commonly asserted form of complexity is called "configural" judgment, in which the diagnostic meaning of one cue depends upon the meaning of other cues (for example, "that tone of voice makes me think 'not suicidal' unless the call comes in the early hours of the morning").

Two reasons for conflict between measured and reported judgment policies have emerged from subsequent research, each with negative implications for the usefulness of regression modeling for "capturing" the wisdom of past decisions. One was the growing realization that combining enormous amounts of information in one's head, as required by such formulae, overwhelms the computational capacity of anyone but an *idiot savant.* A judge trying to implement a complex strategy simply would not be able to do so with great consistency. Indeed, it is difficult to learn and use even a non-configural, weighted sum, decision rule when there are many cues or unusual relationships between the cues and predicted variable (Slovic, 1974).

The second realization that has emerged from clinical judgment research is that simple linear models are extraordinarily powerful predictors. As long as one can identify and measure the attributes relevant to an individual, one can mimic his or her decisions to a large degree with simple models bearing no resemblance to actual cognitive processes. That is, under very general conditions, one can misspecify weights and even combination rules and still do a pretty good job of predicting decisions (Dawes, 1979). Thus, whatever people are doing will look like the application of a simple linear model. In Hoffman's (1960) term, such models are *paramorphic* in that they reproduce the input-output relations of the phenomena they are meant to describe without any guarantee of fidelity to the underlying processes.

Empirically discovering an analytical result by Wilks (1938), Dawes and Corrigan (1974) showed that considerable predictive success is possible without almost any modeling at all. All one has to do is to identify the variables (or attributes) to which a decision maker attends and decide whether they are positively or negatively related to the decision criterion. If these variables are expressed in standard units, they can be given unit weights (+ 1 or − 1, as appropriate). Such a unit weighted model will, under very general conditions, predict decisions as well as a full-blown regression model does.

Thus, a simple substantive theory indicating what variables people care about when making decisions may be all one needs to make reasonably good predictions of their behavior. If some signs encourage a diagnosis or decision and others discourage it, simply counting the number of encouraging and discouraging signs will provide a fair guess at the individual's behavior. The result, however, will be a more modest theory than one can derive by flashy regression modeling.

Obviously, some factors are more important than others. Therefore a theory using importance weights should be more faithful to reality than one using unit weights. However, any unreliability or misspecification of those weights due to poor procedure or multicollinearity reduces their usefulness very quickly. Indeed, models using poorly conceived or executed weighting schemes may succeed in spite of rather than because of their increased sophistication (Fischhoff, Goitein, and Shapira, in press). Thus, while the past seems to be right out there to be understood, our standard statistical procedures do not always tell us what we want to know. If not used carefully, they may mislead us, leaving us less wise than when we started. It is tempting to embrace highly complicated theories in their entirety without realizing that their power comes from very simple underlying notions, rather than from having captured the essence of the past.

Looking for Folly

Searching for wisdom in historic events requires an act of faith, a belief in the existence of recurrent patterns waiting to be discovered. Searching for wisdom in the behavior of historical characters requires a somewhat different act of faith, confidence that our predecessors knew things we do not know. The first of these faiths is grounded in philosophy; it distinguishes those who view history as a social science, not an ideographic study of unique events. The second of these faiths is grounded in charity and modesty. It distinguishes those who hope to see further by standing on the shoulders of those who came before and those satisfied with standing on their faces. Idioms like "those who do not study history are condemned to repeat it" suggest that the latter faith is relatively rare.

An active search for folly is, of course, not without merit. Not only do individuals for whom things do not go right often have a lot of explaining to do, but such explanations are crucial to learning from their experience. By seeing how things went wrong, we hope to make them go right in the future.

Assuming that we know what has happened, we are then in a position to exploit the wisdom of our own hindsight in explaining and evaluating the past behavior of others. On closer examination, however, the advantages of knowing how things turned out may be oversold (Fischhoff, 1975). In hindsight, people consistently exaggerate what could have been anticipated in foresight. They not only tend to view what has happened as being inevitable, but also to view it as having appeared "relatively inevitable" before it happened. People believe that others should have been able to anticipate events much better than was actually the case. They even misremember their own predictions so as to exaggerate in hindsight what they knew in foresight (Fischhoff and Beyth, 1975).

As described by historian Georges Florovsky (1969): "The tendency toward determinism is somehow implied in the method of retrospection itself. In retrospect, we seem to perceive the logic of the events which unfold themselves in a regular or linear fashion according to a recognizable pattern with an alleged inner necessity. So that we get the impression that it really could not have happened otherwise" (p. 369). An apt name for this tendency to view reported outcomes as having been relatively inevitable might be "creeping determinism" in contrast with philosophical determinism, the conscious belief that whatever happens has to happen.

One corollary tendency is to telescope the rate of historical processes, exaggerating the speed with which "inevitable" changes are consummated (Fischer, 1970). For example, people may be able to point to the moment when large landed estates (latifundia) were doomed, without realizing that they took two and a half centuries to disappear. Another is the tendency to remember people as having been much more like their current selves than was actually the case (Yarrow, Campbell, and Burton, 1970). A third may be seen in Barraclough's (1972) critique of the historiography of the ideological roots of Nazism. Looking back from the Third Reich, one can trace its roots to the writings of many authors from whose writings one could not have projected

Nazism. A fourth is to imagine that the participants in a historical situation were fully aware of its eventual importance ("Dear Diary, The Hundred Years' War started today," Fischer, 1970). A fifth is the myth of the critical experiment, unequivocally resolving the conflict between two theories or establishing the validity of one. In fact, "the crucial experiment is seen as crucial only decades later. Theories do not just give up, since a few anomalies are always allowed. Indeed, it is very difficult to defeat a research programme supported by talented and imaginative scientists" (Lakatos, 1970, pp. 157–158).

In the short run, failure to ignore outcome knowledge holds substantial benefits. It is quite flattering to believe, or lead others to believe, that we would have known all along what we could only know with outcome knowledge, that is, that we possess hindsightful foresight. In the long run, however, undetected creeping determinism can seriously impair our ability to judge the past or learn from it.

Consider decision makers who have been caught unprepared by some turn of events and who try to see where they went wrong by recreating their pre-outcome knowledge state of mind. If, in retrospect, the event appears to have seemed relatively likely, they can do little more than berate themselves for not taking action that their knowledge seems to have dictated. They might be said to add the insult of regret to the injury inflicted by the event itself. When second-guessed by a hindsightful observer, their misfortune appears as incompetence, folly, or worse.

In situations where information is limited and indeterminate, occasional surprises and resulting failures are inevitable. It is both unfair and self-defeating to castigate decision makers who have erred in fallible systems, without admitting to that fallibility and doing something to improve the system. According to historian Roberta Wohlstetter (1962), the lesson to be learned from American surprise at Pearl Harbor is that we must "accept the fact of uncertainty and learn to live with it. Since no magic will provide certainty, our plans must work without it" (p. 401).

When we attempt to understand past events, we implicitly test the hypotheses or rules we use both to interpret and to anticipate the world around us. If, in hindsight, we systematically underestimate the surprises that the past held and holds for us, we are subjecting those hypotheses to inordinately weak tests and, presumably, finding little reason to change them. Thus the very outcome knowledge which gives us the feeling that we understand what the past was all about may prevent us from learning anything about it.

Protecting ourselves against this bias requires some understanding of the psychological processes involved in its creation. It appears that when we receive outcome knowledge, we immediately make sense out of it by integrating it into what we already know about the subject. Having made this reinterpretation, the reported outcome now seems a more or less inevitable outgrowth of the reinterpreted situation. "Making sense" out of what we are told about the past is, in turn, so natural that we may be unaware of outcome knowledge having had any effect on us. Even if we are aware of there having been an effect, we may still be unaware of exactly what it was. In trying to reconstruct our foresightful state of mind, we will remain anchored in our hindsightful perspective, leaving the reported outcome too likely looking.

As a result, merely warning people about the dangers of hindsight bias has little effect (Fischhoff, 1977). A more effective manipulation is to force oneself to argue against the inevitability of the reported outcome, that is, try to convince oneself that it might have turned out otherwise. Questioning the validity of the reasons recruited to explain its inevitability might be a good place to start (Koriat, Lichtenstein, and Fischhoff, in press; Slovic and Fischhoff, 1977). Since even this unusual step seems inadequate, one might further try to track down some of the uncertainty surrounding past events in their original form. Are there transcripts of the information reaching the Pearl Harbor Command prior to 7 A.M. on December 7? Is there a notebook showing the stocks you considered before settling on Waltham Industries? Are there diaries capturing Chamberlain's view of Hitler in 1939? An interesting variant was Douglas Freeman's determination not to know about any subsequent events when working on any given period in his definitive biography of Robert E. Lee (Commager, 1965). Although admirable, this strategy does require some naive assumptions about the prevalence of knowledge regarding who surrendered at Appomattox.

Looking at All

Why Look? Study of the past is predicated on the belief that if we look, we will be able to discern some interpretable patterns. Considerable research suggests that this belief is well founded. People seem to have a remarkable ability to find some order or meaning in even randomly produced data. One of the most familiar examples is the gamblers' fallacy. Our feeling is that in flipping a fair coin, four successive "heads" will be followed by a "tail" (Lindman and Edwards, 1961). Thus, in our minds, even random processes are constrained to have orderly internal properties. Kahneman and Tversky (1972) have suggested that of the thirty-two possible sequences of six binary events only one actually looks "random."

Although the gamblers' fallacy is usually cited in the context of piquant but trivial examples, it can also be found in more serious attempts to explain historical events. For example, after cleverly showing that Supreme Court vacancies appear more or less at random (according to a Poisson process), with the probability of at least one vacancy in any given year being .39, Morrison (1977) claimed that:

> [President] Roosevelt announced his plan to pack the Court in February, 1937, shortly after the start of his fifth year in the White House. 1937 was also the year in which he made his first appointment to the Court. That he had this opportunity in 1937 should come as no surprise, because the probability that he would go five consecutive years without appointing one or more justices was but .08, or one chance in

twelve. In other words, when Roosevelt decided to change the Court by creating additional seats, the odds were already eleven to one in his favor that he would be able to name one or more justices by traditional means that very year [pp. 143–144].

However, if vacancies do appear at random, then this reasoning is wrong. It assumes that the probabilistic process creating vacancies, like that governing coin flips, has a memory and a sense of justice, as if it knows that it is moving into the fifth year of the Roosevelt presidency and that it "owes" FDR a vacancy. However, on January 1, 1937, the past four years were history, and the probability of at least one vacancy in the coming year was still .39 (Fischhoff, 1978).

Feller (1968) offers the following anecdote involving even higher stakes: Londoners during the blitz devoted considerable effort to interpreting the pattern of German bombing, developing elaborate theories of where the Germans were aiming (and when to take cover). However, when London was divided up into small, contiguous geographic areas, the frequency distribution of bomb hits per area was almost a perfect approximation of the Poisson distribution. Natural disaster constitutes another category of consequential events where (threatened) lay people see order when experts see randomness (Kates, 1962).

One secret to maintaining such beliefs is failure to keep complete enough records to force ourselves to confront irregularities. Historians acknowledge the role of missing evidence in facilitating their explanations with comments like "the history of the Victorian Age will never be written. We know too much about it. For ignorance is the first requisite of the historian—ignorance which simplifies and clarifies, which selects and omits, with placid perfection unattainable by the highest art" (Strachey, 1918).

Even where records are available and unavoidable, we seem to have a remarkable ability to explain or provide a causal interpretation for whatever we see. When events are produced by probabilistic processes with intuitive properties, random variation may not even occur to us as a potential hypothesis. For example, the fact that athletes chastized for poor performance tend to do better the next time out fits our naive theories of reward and punishment. This handy explanation blinds us to the possibility that the improvement is due instead to regression to those players' mean performance (Furby, 1973; Kahneman and Tversky, 1973).

Fama (1965) has forcefully argued that the fluctuations of stockmarket prices are best understood as reflecting a random walk process. Random walks, however, have even more unintuitive properties than the binary processes to which they are formally related (Carlsson, 1972). As a result, we find that market analysts have an explanation for every change in price, whether purposeful or not. Some explanations are inconsistent: for example, when the market rises following good economic news, it is said to be responding to the news; if it falls, that is explained by saying that the good news had already been discounted. Other explanations seem to deny the possibility of any random factor—for example, that ultimate fudge factor, the "technical adjustment."

The pseudo-power of our explanations can be illustrated by analogy with regression analysis. Given a set of events and a sufficiently large or rich set of possible explanatory factors, one can always derive post-dictions or explanations to any desired degree of tightness. In regression terms, by expanding the set of independent variables one can always find a set of predictors with any desired correlation with the independent variable. The price one pays for overfitting is, of course, shrinkage, failure of the derived rule to work on a new sample of cases. The frequency and vehemence of methodological warnings against overfitting suggest that correlational overkill is a bias that is quite resistant to even extended professional training (for references, see Fischhoff and Slovic, in press).

One way of thinking of an overfitted theory is like a suit tailored so precisely to one individual in one particular pose that it will not fit anyone else or even that same individual in the future or even in the present if new evidence about him comes to light (for instance, he lets out his breath to reveal a potbelly). An historian who had built an airtight case accounting for all available evidence in explaining how the Bolsheviks won might be in a sad position were the USSR to release suppressed documents showing that the Mensheviks were more serious adversaries than had previously been thought. The price investment analysts pay for overfitting is their long-run failure to predict any better than market averages (Dreman, in press)—although the cynic might say that they actually make their living through the generation of hope (and commissions).

Overfitting works because of capitalization on chance fluctuations. If measurement is sufficiently fine, two cases differing on one variable will also differ on almost any other variable one chooses to name. As a result, one can calculate a non-zero (actually, in this case, perfect) correlation between the two variables and derive an "interesting" substantive theory. Processes analogous to this two-dimensional case work with any m observations in the n-space defined by our set of possible explanatory concepts.

In these examples, the data are fixed and undeniable, while the set of possible explanations is relatively unbounded; one hunts until one finds an explanation that fits. Another popular form of capitalization on chance leaves the set of explanations fixed (usually at one candidate) and sifts through data until supporting evidence is found. While the crasser forms of this procedure are well known, others are more subtle and even somewhat ambiguous in their characterization. For example, you run an experiment and fail to receive an anticipated result. Thinking about it, you note an element of your procedure that might have mitigated the effect of the manipulated variable. You correct that; again no result, but again a possible problem. Finally, you (or your subjects) get it right and the anticipated effect is obtained. Now, is it right to perform your statistical test on that n'th sample (for which it shows significance) or the whole lot of them? Had you done the right experiment first, the question would not even have arisen. Or, as a toxicologist, you are "certain" that exposure to Chemical X is bad for one's health, so you compare workers who do and do not work with it in a particular plant for bladder cancer, but still no effect. So you try intestinal cancer, emphysema, dizziness, . . . , until you finally get a significant difference in skin cancer. Is that difference meaningful? Of course, the way to test these explanations or theories is by replication on new samples. That step, unfortunately, is seldom taken and often not possible for technical or ethical reasons (Tukey, 1977).

Related complications can arise even with fixed theories and data sets. Diaconis (1978) notes the difficulty of evaluating the surprisingness of ESP results, even in the rare cases in which they have been obtained in moderately supervised settings, because the definition of the sought event keeps shifting. "A major key to B.D.'s success was that he did not specify in advance the result to be considered surprising. The odds against a coincidence *of some sort* are dramatically less than those against any prespecified *particular one* of them" (p. 132).

Tufte and Sun (1975) discovered that the existence or non-existence of bellwether precincts depends upon the creativity and flexibility allowed in defining the event (for what office, in what elections, how good is good, are precincts that miss consistently to be included?). They are commonly believed to exist because we have an uncommonly good ability to find a signal even in total noise.

Have We Seen Enough? Given that we are almost assured of finding something interpretable when we look at the past, our next question becomes "have we understood it?" The hindsight research described earlier suggests that we are not only quick to find order, but also poised to feel that we knew it all along in some way, or would have been able to predict the result had we been asked in time. Indeed, the ease with which we discount the informativeness of anything we are told makes it surprising that we ever ask the past, or any other source, many questions. This tendency is aggravated by tendencies (1) not to realize how little we know or are told, leaving us unaware of what questions we should be asking in search of surprising answers (Fischhoff, Slovic, and Lichtenstein, 1977, 1978) and (2) to draw far-reaching conclusions from even small amounts of unreliable data (Kahneman and Tversky, 1973; Tversky and Kahneman, 1971).

Any propensity to look no further is encouraged by the norm of reporting history as a good story, with all the relevant details neatly accounted for and the uncertainty surrounding the event prior to its consummation summarily buried, along with any confusion the author may have felt (Gallie, 1964; Nowell-Smith, 1970). Just one of the secrets to doing this is revealed by Tawney (1961). "Historians give an appearance of inevitability to an existing order by dragging into prominence the forces which have triumphed and thrusting into the background those which they have swallowed up" (p. 177).

Although an intuitively appealing goal, the construction of coherent narratives exposes the reader to some interesting biases. A completed narrative consists of a series of somewhat independent links, each fairly well established. The truth of the narrative depends upon the truth of the links. Generally, the more links there are, the more detail in each link, the less likely the story is to be correct in its entirety. However, Slovic, Fischhoff, and Lichtenstein (1976) have found that adding detail to an event description can increase its perceived probability of occurrence, evidently by increasing its thematic unity. Bar Hillel (1973) found that people consistently exaggerate the probability of the conjunction of a series of likely events. For example, her subjects generally preferred a situation in which they would receive a prize if seven independent events each with a probability of .90 were to occur to a situation in which they would get the same prize if a fair coin fell on "heads." The probability of the compound event is less than .50, whereas the probability of the single event is .50. In other words, uncertainty seems to accumulate at much too slow a rate.

What happens if the sequence includes one or a few weak or unlikely links? The probability of its weakest link should set an upper limit on the probability of an entire narrative. Coherent judgments, however, may be compensatory, with the coherence of strong links "evening out" the incoherence of weak links. This effect is exploited by attorneys who bury the weakest link in their arguments near the beginning of their summations and finish with a flurry of convincing, uncontestable arguments.

Coles (1973) presents a delicious example of the overall coherence of a story obscurring the unlikelihood of its links: Freud's most serious attempt at psychohistory was his biography of Leonardo DeVinci. For years, Freud had sought the secret to understanding Leonardo, whose childhood and youth were basically unknown. Finally, he discovered a reference by Leonardo to a recurrent memory of a vulture touching his lips while he was in the cradle. Noting the identity of the Egyptian hieroglyphs for "vulture" and "mother" and other circumstantial evidence, Freud went on the build an imposing and coherent analysis of Leonardo. While compiling the definitive edition of Freud's works, however, the editor discovered that the German translation of Leonardo's recollection (originally in Italian) which Freud had used was in error, and that it was a kite and not a vulture which had stroked his lips. Despite having the key to Freud's analysis destroyed, the editor's decided that the remaining edifice was strong enough to stand alone. As Hexter (1971) observed, "Partly because writing bad history is pretty easy, writing very good history is rare" (p. 59).

Conclusion

What general lessons can we learn about the study of the past, beyond the fact that understanding is more elusive than may often be acknowledged?

Presentism. Inevitably, we are all captives of our present personal perspective. We know things that those living in the past did not. We use analytical categories (such as feudalism, Hundred Years War) that are meaningful only in retrospect (Brown, 1974). We have our own points to prove when interpreting a past which is never sufficiently unambiguous to avoid the imposition of our ideological perspective (Degler, 1976). Historians do "play new tricks on the dead in every generation" (Becker, 1935).

There is no proven antidote to presentism. Some partial remedies can be generalized from the discussion of how to avoid hindsight bias when second-guessing the past. Others appear in almost any text devoted to the training of historians. Perhaps the most general messages seem to be (1) knowing ourselves and the present as well as possible; "the historian who is most conscious of his own situation is also most capable of transcending it" (Croce, quoted in Carr, 1961, p. 44); and (2) being as charitable as possible to our predecessors; "the historian is not a judge, still less a hanging judge" (Knowles, quoted in Marwick, 1970, p. 101).

Methodism. In addition to the prison of our own time, we often further restrict our own perspective by voluntarily adopting the blinders that accompany strict adherence to a single scientific method. Even when used judiciously, no one method is adequate for answering many of the questions we put to the past. Each tells us something and misleads us somewhat. When we do not know how to get the right answer to a question, an alternative epistemology is needed: use as broad a range of techniques or perspectives as possible, each of which enables us to avoid certain kinds of mistakes. This means a sort of interdisciplinary cooperation and respect different from that encountered in most attempts to comingle two approaches. Matches or mismatches like psychohistory too often are attempted by advocates insensitive to the pitfalls in their adopted fields (Fischhoff, in press). Hexter (1971) describes the historians involved in some such adventures as "rats jumping aboard intellectually sinking ships" (p.10).

Learning. Returning to Benson, if we want the past to serve the future, we cannot treat it in isolation. The rules we use to explain the past must also be those we use to predict the future. We must cumulate our experience with a careful eye to all relevant tests of our hypotheses. One aspect of doing this is compiling records that can be subjected to systematic statistical analysis; a second is keeping track of the deliberations preceding our own decisions, realizing that the present will soon be past and that a well-preserved record is the best remedy to hindsight bias; a third is to make predictions which can be evaluated. One disturbing lesson from Three Mile Island is that it is not entirely clear what that ostensibly diagnostic event told us about the validity of the Reactor Safety Study (U.S. Nuclear Regulatory Commission, 1975) which attempted to assess the risks from nuclear power; a fourth is to get a better idea of the validity of our own feelings of confidence, insofar as confidence in present knowledge controls our pursuit of new information and interpretation (Fischhoff, Slovic, and Lichtenstein, 1977). Thus we want to structure our lives so as to facilitate learning.

Indeterminacy. In the end, though, there may be no answers to many of the questions we are posing. Some are ill-formed. Others just cannot be answered with existing or possible tools. As much as we would like to know "how the pros do it," there may be no way statistically to model experts' judgmental policies to the desired degree of precision with realistic stimuli. Our theories are often of "such complexity that no single quantitative work could even begin to text their validity" (O'Leary and others, 1974, p. 228). When groups we wish to compare on one variable also differ on another, there is no logically sound procedure for equating them on that nuisance variable (Meehl, 1970). When we have tried many possible explanations on a fixed set of data, there is no ironclad way of knowing just how many degrees of freedom we have used up, just how far we have capitalized on chance (Campbell, 1975). When we use multiple approaches, the knowledge they produce never converges neatly. In the end, we may have to adopt Trevelyan's philosophical perspective that "several imperfect readings of history are better than none at all" (cited in Marwick, 1970, p. 57).

References

Bar-Hillel, M. "On the Subjective Probability of Compound Events." *Organizational Behavior and Human Performance,* 1973, *9,* 396–406.

Barraclough, G. "Mandarins and Nazis." *New York Review of Books,* 1972, *19* (6), 37–42.

Becker, C. "Everyman His Own Historian." *American Historical Review,* 1935, *40,* 221–236.

Benson, L. *Toward the Scientific Study of History: Selected Essays.* Philadelphia: Lippincott, 1972.

Brown, E. A. R. "The Tyranny of a Construct: Feudalism and Historians of Medieval Europe." *American Historical Review,* 1974, *79,* 1063–1088.

Campbell, D. T. " 'Degrees of Freedom' and the Case Study." *Comparative Political Studies,* 1975, *8,* 178–193.

Carlsson, G. "Random Walk Effects in Behavioral Data." *Behavioral Science,* 1972, *17,* 430–437.

Carr, E. H. *What Is History?* London, Macmillan, 1961.

Coles, R. "Shrinking History." *New York Review of Books,* Part I in Feb. 22, 1973, *20,* pp. 15–21 and Part II in Mar. 8, 1973, *20,* pp. 25–29.

Commager, H. S. *The Nature and Study of History.* Columbus, Ohio: Merrill, 1965.

Dawes, R. M. "The Robust Beauty of Improper Linear Models in Decision Making." *American Psychologist,* 1979, *34,* 571–582.

Dawes, R. M., and Corrigan, B. "Linear Models in Decision Making." *Psychological Bulletin,* 1974, *81* (2), 95–106.

Degler, C. N. "Why Historians Change Their Minds." *Pacific Historical Review,* 1976, *48,* 167–189.

Diaconis, P. "Statistical Problems in ESP Research." *Science,* 1978, *201,* 131–136.

Dreman, D. *Contrarian Investment Strategy.* New York: Random House, in press.

Fama, E. F. "Random Walks in Stock Market Prices." *Financial Analysts Journal,* 1965, *21,* 55–60.

Feller, W. *An Introduction to Probability Theory and Its Applications.* (3rd ed.) Vol. 1. New York: Harper & Row, 1968.

Fischer, D. H. *Historian's Fallacies.* New York: Harper & Row, 1970.

Fischhoff, B. "Hindsight ≠ Foresight: The Effect of Outcome Knowledge on Judgment Under Uncertainty." *Journal of Experimental Psychology: Human Perception and Performance,* 1975, *1,* 288–299.

Fischhoff, B. "Perceived Informativeness of Facts." *Journal of Experimental Psychology: Human Perception and Performance,* 1977, *3,* 349–358.

Fischhoff, B. "Intuitive Use of Formal Models. A Comment on Morrison's 'Quantitative Models in History.' " *History and Theory,* 1978, *17,* 207–210.

Fischhoff, B. "No Man Is a Discipline." In J. Harvey (Ed.), *Cognition, Social Behavior, and the Environment.* Hillsdale, N.J.: Erlbaum, in press.

Fischhoff, B., and Beyth, R. " 'I Knew It Would Happen'—Remembered Probabilities of Once-Future Things." *Organizational Behavior and Human Performance,* 1975, *13,* 1-16.
Fischhoff, B., Goitein, B., and Shapira, Z. "The Experienced Utility of Expected Utility Approaches." In N. Feather (Ed.), *Expectancy, Incentive, and Action.* Hillsdale, N.J.: Erlbaum, in press.
Fischhoff, B., and Slovic, P. "A Little Learning . . . : Confidence in Multicue Judgment." *Attention and Performance,* VIII, in press.
Fischhoff, B., Slovic, P., and Lichtenstein, S. "Knowing with Certainty: The Appropriateness of Extreme Confidence." *Journal of Experimental Psychology: Human Perception and Performance,* 1977, *3,* 552-564.
Fischhoff, B., Slovic, P., and Lichtenstein, S. "Fault Trees: Sensitivity of Estimated Failure Probabilities to Problem Representation." *Journal of Experimental Psychology: Human Perception and Performance,* 1978, *4,* 330-344.
Florovsky, G. "The Study of the Past." In R. H. Nash (Ed.), *Ideas of History.* Vol. 2. New York: Dutton, 1969.
Furby, L. "Interpreting Regression Toward the Mean in Developmental Research." *Developmental Psychology,* 1973, *8,* 172-179.
Gallie, W. B. *Philosophy and the Historical Understanding.* London: Chatto and Windus, 1964.
Goldberg, L. R. "Simple Models or Simple Processes? Some Research on Clinical Judgments." *American Psychologist,* 1968, *23,* 483-496.
Goldberg, L. R. "Man Versus Model of Man: A Rationale, Plus Some Evidence, for a Method of Improving on Clinical Inference." *Psychological Bulletin,* 1970, *73,* 422-432.
Hexter, J. H. *The History Primer.* New York: Basic Books, 1971.
Hoffman, P. J. "The Paramorphic Representation of Clinical Judgment." *Psychological Bulletin,* 1960, *47,* 116-131.
Kahneman, D., and Tversky, A. "Subjective Probability: A Judgment of Representativeness." *Cognitive Psychology,* 1972, *3,* 430-454.
Kahneman, D., and Tversky, A. "On the Psychology of Prediction." *Psychological Review,* 1973, *80,* 237-251.
Kates, R. W. *Hazard and Choice Perception in Flood Plain Management.* Research Paper No. 78. Chicago: University of Chicago, Department of Geography, 1962.
Koriat, A., Lichtenstein, S., and Fischhoff, B. "Reasons for Confidence." *Journal of Experimental Psychology: Human Learning and Memory,* in press.
Lakatos, I. "Falsification and Scientific Research Programmes." In I. Lakatos and A. Musgrave (Eds.), *Criticism and the Growth of Scientific Knowledge.* Cambridge: Cambridge University Press, 1970.
Lindman, H. G., and Edwards, W. "Supplementary Report: Unlearning the Gamblers' Fallacy." *Journal of Experimental Psychology,* 1961, *62,* 630.
Marwick, A. *The Nature of History.* London: Macmillan, 1970.
Meehl, P. E. "Nuisance Variables and the Ex Post Facto Design." In M. Radner and S. Winokur (Eds.), *Minnesota Studies in the Philosophy of Science.* Minneapolis: University of Minnesota Press, 1970.
Morrison, R. J. "Franklin D. Roosevelt and the Supreme Court: An Example of the Use of Probability Theory in Political History." *History and Theory,* 1977, *16,* 137-146.
Nowell-Smith, P. H. "Historical Explanation." In H. E. Kiefer and M. K. Munitz (Eds.), *Mind, Science, and History.* Albany: State University of New York Press, 1970.
O'Leary, M. K., Coplin, W. D., Shapiro, H. B., and Dean, D. "The Quest for Relevance." *International Studies Quarterly,* 1974, *18,* 211-237.
Slovic, P. "Hypothesis Testing in the Learning of Positive and Negative Linear Functions." *Organizational Behavior and Human Performan,e,* 1974, *11,* 368-376.

Slovic, P., and Fischhoff, B. "On the Psychology of Experimental Surprises." *Journal of Experimental Psychology: Human Perception and Performance,* 1977, *3,* 544–551.

Slovic, P., Fischhoff, B., and Lichtenstein, S. "Cognitive Processes and Societal Risk Taking." In J. S. Carroll and J. W. Payne (Eds.), *Cognition and Social Behavior.* Hillsdale, N.J.: Erlbaum, 1976.

Slovic, P., and Lichtenstein, S. "Comparison of Bayesian and Regression Approaches to the Study of Information Processing in Judgment." *Organizational Behavior and Human Performance,* 1971, *6,* 649–744.

Strachey, L. *Eminent Victorians.* New York: Putnam's, 1918.

Tawney, R. H. *The Agrarian Problem in the Sixteenth Century.* New York: Franklin, 1961.

Tufte, E. R., and Sun, R. A. "Are There Bellwether Electoral Districts?" *The Public Opinion Quarterly,* 1975, *39,* 1–18.

Tukey, J. W. "Some Thoughts on Clinical Trials, Especially Problems of Multiplicity." *Science,* 1977, *198,* 679–690.

Tversky, A., and Kahneman, D. "The Belief in the 'Law of Small Numbers.' " *Psychological Bulletin,* 1971, *76,* 105–110.

Wilks, S. S. "Weighting Systems for Linear Functions of Correlated Variables When There Is No Dependent Variable." *Psychometrika,* 1938, *3,* 23–40.

Wohlstetter, R. *Pearl Harbor: Warnings and Decision.* Stanford, Calif.: Stanford University Press, 1962.

Yarrow, M., Campbell, J. D., and Burton, R. V. "Recollections of Childhood: A Study of the Retrospective Method." *Monographs of the Society for Research in Child Development,* 1970, *35* (5).

*Baruch Fischhoff is research scientist at Decision Research, a branch of Perceptronics, 1201 Oak Street, Eugene, Oregon 97401.
His primary interests include the psychology of individual judgment and decision making, subjective aspects of formal decision making procedures, the management of technological hazards, and historical judgment.*

Index

G

H

J

K

L

M

N

New Directions Quarterly Sourcebooks

New Directions for Methodology of Social and Behavioral Science is one of several distinct series of quarterly sourcebooks published by Jossey-Bass. The sourcebooks in each series are designed to serve both as *convenient compendiums* of the latest knowledge and practical experience on their topics and as *long-life reference tools.*

One-year, four-sourcebook subscriptions for each series cost $18 for individuals (when paid by personal check) and $30 for institutions, libraries, and agencies. Single copies of earlier sourcebooks are available at $6.95 each *prepaid* (or $7.95 each when *billed*).

A complete listing is given below of current and past sourcebooks in the *New Directions for Methodology of Social and Behavioral Science* series. The titles and editors-in-chief of the other series are also listed. To subscribe, or to receive further information, write: New Directions Subscriptions, Jossey-Bass Inc., Publishers, 433 California Street, San Francisco, California 94104.

New Directions for Methodology of Social and Behavioral Science
Donald W. Fiske, Editor-in-Chief
1979–1980: 1. *Unobtrusive Measurement Today,* Lee Sechrest
2. *Methods for Studying Person-Situation Interactions,* Lynn R. Kahle
3. *Realizations of Brunswik's Representative Design,* Kenneth R. Hammond, Nancy E. Wascoe

New Directions for Child Development
William Damon, Editor-in-Chief

New Directions for College Learning Assistance
Kurt V. Lauridsen, Editor-in-Chief

New Directions for Community Colleges
Arthur M. Cohen, Editor-in-Chief
Florence B. Brawer, Associate Editor

New Directions for Continuing Education
Alan B. Knox, Editor-in-Chief

New Directions for Exceptional Children
James J. Gallagher, Editor-in-Chief

New Directions for Experiential Learning
Morris T. Keeton and Pamela J. Tate, Editors-in-Chief

New Directions for Higher Education
JB Lon Hefferlin, Editor-in-Chief

New Directions for Institutional Advancement
A. Westley Rowland, Editor-in-Chief

New Directions for Institutional Research
Marvin W. Peterson, Editor-in-Chief

New Directions for Mental Health Services
H. Richard Lamb, Editor-in-Chief

New Directions for Program Evaluation
Scarvia B. Anderson, Editor-in-Chief

New Directions for Student Services
Ursula Delworth and Gary R. Hanson, Editors-in-Chief

New Directions for Teaching and Learning
Kenneth E. Eble and John Noonan, Editors-in-Chief

New Directions for Testing and Measurement
William B. Schrader, Editor-in-Chief